A MUSLIM SAGE AMONG PEERS

Fethullah Gülen in Dialogue with Christians

A MUSLIM SAGE AMONG PEERS
Fethullah Gülen in Dialogue with Christians

Edited by
John D. Barton

NEW JERSEY ● LONDON ● FRANKFURT ● CAIRO ● JAKARTA

BLUE DOME

NEW JERSEY

Published by Blue Dome Press
335 Clifton Avenue, Clifton, NJ 07011

www.bluedomepress.com

Library of Congress Cataloging-in-Publication Data Available

ISBN: 978-168206-018-6

Contents

Dedication

I am grateful for good friends who have made my journey in Christian/Muslim interactions so interesting and enjoyable. Special thanks to Saeed Khan, Keith Huey, Ali Ngobi, Hakan Yildiz, Salih Ozdemir, Yasir Bilgin, Ahmed Taha, Amal Bahloul, Hichem Aouina, Mustafa Akyol, Michal Muelenberg, Sondos Kholaki, Atilla Kahveci, Edina Lekovic, Asim Buyuksoy, Jihad Turk, Ozgur Koca, my friends at Bayan Claremont, and many others.

I am also grateful to the editorial assistance provided by Falon Opsahl who, in the middle of the project, became Falon Barton by marrying my son. I could not ask for a better editor or, more importantly, daughter-in-law!

Editor's Introduction

The need for well-informed and nuanced dialogue between Christians and Muslims has never been more important.

Roughly half of the world's population self-identifies as either Christian or Muslim, and both religions are witnessing remarkable levels of growth.[1] In addition, and maybe unsurprisingly, many of the world's most significant challenges surface along the geographical and ideological borders of these two diverse communities. Religion is not the only relevant category through which to consider geopolitical issues, but religious forces profoundly reflect and affect the cultural, sociopolitical, economic, and psychological factors that shape our world.[2] As we long for peace in our shared global spaces, therefore, positive interactions between the world's largest religious groups are imperative.

This volume contributes to such efforts by putting various Christian leaders and organizations in dialogue with the Turkish sage and scholar, Fethullah Gülen. Gülen has been called "one of the world's most important Muslim figures."[3] Some may challenge such a designation, but its claim is bolstered by the sheer number of publications about him by advocates, crit-

---

[1]   Recent Pew reports compare the growth of different religions and find that Islam is outpacing all other major traditions and, when projected out, will nearly overtake Christianity as the world's largest religion by 2050. Of course, such projections are complex and debated and must grapple with variables such as immigration patterns, fertility rates, ideological and socioeconomic impacts. Regardless, the fact that these two religions are currently growing and interacting with one another in increasing ways is indisputable.   See http://www.pewforum.org/2015/04/02/religious-projections-2010-2050/.

[2]   For a recent exploration of how religion and the forces of globalization interact and affect one another, see Miroslav Volf *Flourishing: Why We Need Religion in a Globalized World* (New Haven: Yale University Press, 2015).

[3]   http://www.economist.com/node/10808408?story_id=10808408

ics, and "neutral" observers alike.[4] Furthermore, whether one is supportive or critical of Gülen, it would be difficult to exaggerate the global reach of the amorphous *Hizmet* movement that he inspires with its vast international philanthropic and educational initiatives.

On the other hand, it would also be difficult to exaggerate the level of controversy that orbits Gülen and his legacy. During his decades of public leadership, there have always been critics who consider him a subversive figure in Turkey. Such accusations have become more acute and visible since Turkey's failed *coup d'état* in July 2016. In fact, while this volume imagines Gülen in dialogue with various "peers," it is clear that the "reclusive cleric" in Pennsylvania also has an increasing number of critics, even enemies. Moreover, the severity of the Turkish government's recent crackdown on dissidents, including many *Hizmet* sympathizers, has instigated substantial changes in the movement worldwide and it is not yet clear how things will play out. Regardless of one's perspectives on the cultural and political issues, the whole situation calls for increased vigilance and prayer.

This volume does not directly address the situation in Turkey and, in fact, most of the essays included here were presented and written long before the current tensions in Turkey became so acute. What this volume does do, however, is seek to draw attention to aspects of Gülen's interfaith work through the years and put it in dialogue with various strands of western Christianity. Toward that end, the essays herein put Gülen and the *Hizmet* movement in dialogue with Christian theologians, philosophers and organizations concerning areas of shared interest. The Christian voices represented in these constructed dialogues are diverse: contemporary and historical, Catholic and Protestant, theological and pragmatic. While all of the essays explore overlaps and similarities between Gülen and these dialogue partners, they also bring to the surface differences and critical assessments. The result is a multi-faceted conversation that invites us all into deeper levels of historical and theological imagination, self-reflection, and collaborative service.

---

[4] An example of an attempt at a third-party, objective assessment of Gülen and *Hizmet* is M. Hakan Yavuz, *Toward an Islamic Enlightenment: The Gülen Movement* (Oxford University Press, 2013).

In the end, while keeping Turkey and all of its citizens and leaders in prayer, it is hoped that this volume will provide one more contribution, modest as it may be, to a larger discourse and a world desperate for peace, *insha'Allah.*

******

The essays in this volume are arranged in two broad categories. Part One ("Gülen Among Contemporary Peers") places Gülen and *Hizmet* in dialogue with Christian leaders, organizations or events concurrent with Gülen's own life and work. Part Two ("Gülen Among Historical Peers") imagines him and *Hizmet* in dialogue with various Christian leaders or movements from other historical eras. Below is a brief introduction of the essays in the order that they appear.

Part One includes six essays that present "discussions" between Gülen and certain contemporary peers about various facets of moral and philosophical thought that have implications for faith, service, and dialogue. The first of these is an insightful essay by Daniel W. Skubik in which he compares Gülen's moral thought with that of the preeminent Anglophone philosopher Alasdair MacIntyre. After a brief description of the impasse common in modern objectivist debates that focus on ethical action (*What should we do?*), Skubik presents Gülen and MacIntyre as both drawing on more ancient, Aristotelean, teleological notions of agent virtue (*Who should we be?*). Skubik demonstrates that while both seek universal values that overlap, both also work from within a specific religious tradition that involves distinct metaphysical commitments: MacIntyre from a Christian Thomistic framework and Gülen from a Sufi-influenced Sunni framework. Skubik then weaves together MacIntyre's thought with Gülen's influence through a fascinating discussion of one of the "ticklish" issues in virtue ethics: whether one can reasonably speak of the virtues, vices, and moral responsibilities of institutions. Drawing on MacIntyre's distinction between internal and external goods, Skubik answers this question affirmatively and finds a specific example of a virtuous financial institution in a Gülen-inspired, Turkish-based bank. Bank Asya is materially successful while offering a virtuous alternative to the strictly secular, interest-bearing, debt-expanding standards common in many financial sectors. Skubik concludes by showing his own philosophical hand more fully: "[O]nly when institutions are virtuous will the virtue of the people be able to flourish. Individuals cannot thrive alone." In the end, Skubik presents Gülen and MacIntyre as distinct but compatible voices that explore ways to imagine and corporately embody virtue through deliberate communities of faith.

In chapter 2, Simon Robinson compares the philosophy and practice of peacebuilding in the work of Gülen with that of the Mennonite scholar and activist, J.P. Lederach. Robinson finds Gülen and Lederach to be "kindred spirits" based on their shared conviction that peacebuilding should be located "at the heart of every debate and action." Nevertheless, Robinson immediately locates significant differences in the two thinkers' definitions, contexts and approaches to peacebuilding. According to Robinson, Gülen provides a more specifically theological (Islamic) approach to peacebuilding based on our accountability to God and responsibility for God's diverse creation. With this theological inspiration, the *Hizmet* movement seeks to address the "three giants" of ignorance, poverty and disunity through deliberate action-oriented forms of education, development and dialogue. In short, Robinson presents Gülen as representing theologically-inspired, programmatic and institutionalized approaches to peacebuilding. Robinson then considers Lederach's approaches as reflected in his peacebuilding work in places such as Somalia, Nicaragua and Northern Ireland, and his academic work in books such as *Moral Imagination.* In contrast to Gülen, Lederach does not privilege programmatic initiatives and does not explicitly reference a theological framework or even his own Mennonite background. Lederach's approach is more generally philosophical and emphasizes relational, non-linear and creative processes. Lederach works from the assumption that conflict is inevitable and thus frames peacebuilding less in terms of programmatic solutions and more in terms of "a journey of managed uncertainty" in light of the alterity of the other and the plurality of narratives. Through various comparisons and contrasts, Robinson provides useful reference points and insights not only for understanding these two individuals and their influence, but for the shared pursuit of peace for our broken world.

Chapter 3 marks a shift in both thematic content and theological context as David P. Capes explores different meanings of "tolerance" through a dialogue between Gülen and the late Baptist theologian A. J. Conyers (1946-2004). Conyers influentially critiques secular notions of tolerance by stating that they assume an artificial division between public and private spheres that result in the marginalization of religion. This modern marginalization and privatization of religion actually ends up creating new forms of intolerance that privilege secular power and materialism. In light of this, Conyers reimagines the notion itself and presents an "authentic tolerance" that is not confined to the private realm but is framed by Christian theology and virtues such as humility, hospitality, dialogue, and love. Conyers and Gülen clearly represent different cultural and religious orientations and there is no evidence of direct influences between them. Nevertheless, Capes finds "amazing resonance" when comparing them on the issue of tolerance. While Conyers draws on "powerful fact of the incarnation" and Gülen draws on Qur'anic materials and the examples of the Prophet, both find deep resources within their respective traditions to promote peace, freedom for the other, and the interrelatedness of all things. Both also discuss the limits of tolerance when it is pursued in submission to virtues such as justice and love. Interestingly, a primary difference that Capes highlights is the way Gülen explicitly aligns notions of tolerance with practices of forgiveness and non-retaliation, whereas Conyers does not. Capes suggests that this difference may reflect the fact that Conyers worked primarily in academic and insulated ecclesial settings while Gülen's thought evolved through experiences of struggle and injustice. Regardless, in the end Capes suggests that if the two had been able to meet, they would have discovered in each other allies for peace and a mutually-benefitting friendship.

The essays in chapters 4 and 5 reflect another shift in context as Gülen is put into dialogue with retired Pope Benedict XVI and then, more abstractly, with the Second Vatican council's *Nostra Aetate* document. Fr. Thomas Michel sets up a "scholarly conversation" between Gülen and the former pope on topics such as the relationship between religion and democracy, religious freedom, and justice and holistic development. Michel's goal is to give attention to the diverse yet compatible voices of these two religious leaders as they address complex issues that confront us all. While different terms are used and different contexts addressed—for example, Gülen often addresses the topics with Turkey in mind, while the pope addresses them more generally— many shared and overlapping values surface. Both contrast the transient and changing forms of democracy with religion's pursuit of eternal realities. Both note how this distinction encourages us to consider the different expectations and roles that should be associated with religion and democracy. Both leaders are clear that the religions they represent do not require a specific form of government *per se*, but both also find democracy to be especially compatible with the needs of the globalized world and the unchanging values of justice, equity, the common good, and the dignity of all people, especially the most vulnerable. Furthermore, both discuss how their religions promote freedom and holistic development. In the end, Gülen and Pope Benedict XVI are presented as promoting certain kinds of "Islamic humanism" and "Christian humanism" respectively, thus helping us imagine how the voices of these two communities might work together in God-honoring ways to contribute to justice and human flourishing.

Next Salih Yücel makes a strong case that interfaith dialogue needs to be proactively institutionalized to have full effect. To make his point, he compares and contrasts the interfaith work of Gülen with Vatican II's *Nostra Aetate*, or "Declaration on the Relation of the Church with Non-Christian Religions."[5] While Yücel celebrates the significance and the substantial influence of *Nostra Aetate*, he also notes that Gülen's forerunner Said Nursi offered progressive proposals for interfaith dialogue and cooperation fifty years before the Second Vatican Council, and even then was merely reflecting a value that dates back to Islam's inception. While the circumstances of the early Turkish republic limited Nursi's ability to implement his proposals, Gülen was soon able to pick up the mantel and Yücel traces the extensive influence of Gülen's interfaith work in Turkey and around the world. Despite the criticisms Gülen receives from both secularists and Islamists, Yücel finds his interfaith work to be "remark-

---

5   *Nostra Aetate* is Latin for "in our time" which are the first words of the Declaration's Latin text and is often used as an informal title of the document.

able and bold" especially when put in contrast with other Christian and Muslim approaches that are characterized by aggressive polemics or limiting conditions. Gülen's approach, by contrast, promotes unconditional, non-proselytizing, and nonpolemical dialogue that centers on shared humanity, service, and love. Central to his thesis, Yücel also highlights the way Gülen has succeeded in institutionalizing these efforts. The institutionalizing of interfaith initiatives makes them, Yücel argues, more effective. Acknowledging the geopolitical challenges of today's world, Yücel finds hope in the evolving legacies of Fethullah Gülen, Vatican II, and similarly-minded movements and initiatives which seek global peace.

In the final essay in Part One, Özgür Koca compares and contrasts Gülen's understandings and practices of spirituality with that of renowned Catholic monk, author, and social activist, Thomas Merton. Koca first notes some of the differences between the two. For example, Merton draws on a wider array of resources including the philosophies of Marxism and Existentialism, and the philosophical traditions of the East, notably Buddhism. Gülen, on the other hand, remains more focused on the sources and traditions of Islam. Nevertheless, Koca finds overlapping ideas which make enriching comparison possible. Both offer "novel approaches" which combine rich traditions of spiritual thought and practice with social activism. Koca leads us on a thoughtful exploration of the thought and practice of these two great exemplars, noting the themes of solitude, self-reflection, self-discipline, and nuanced asceticism, and how these thoughts and practices cause both of them to move beyond the walls of monastery and Sufi order, respectively. In short, both Gülen and Merton allow us to imagine the deep resources of spiritual contemplation and practice in non-escapist ways that provide insight and energy for the work of social engagement.

Transitioning to Part Two of the collection, three essays put Gülen in dialogue with various Christian thinkers and institutions that are not his historical contemporaries. These essays, therefore, require more historical imagination, but the results are no less insightful or relevant. In chapter 7, Pim Valkenberg puts Gülen in dialogue with the early-modern Dutch humanist Desiderius Erasmus. In doing so, Valkenberg also offers both empathetic support and constructive criticism for the Gülen Movement. Drawing on several Dutch conferences from recent years that consider the comparison of these two figures, Valkenberg sketches some of the similarities between Gülen and Erasmus with regard to peace initiatives and education, but also presents an account of an intriguing difference: Erasmus' Christian motives and assumptions were often on clear display despite his legacy as one of the first great modern humanists, while the clear Islamic motives of Gülen and his followers often remain implicit at best. In reply to the siege of Vienna by the Ottomans in 1529, Erasmus wrote a treatise calling for a united Christian front to stand against the Muslim invaders. While this "front" was conceived more evangelistically than militarily, Valkenberg's primary observation is that Erasmus' call for a united Christian front first required respectful dialogue and peacebuilding among the warring Catholics and Protestants of his day. But Erasmus' Christian humanism, it seems, did not propose such dialogue or extend the same respect to Muslims. In this sense, therefore, Valkenberg considers Gülen a "better bridge-builder" since his efforts explicitly promote respect and peaceful dialogue not only between diverse Muslim populations but also with Christians and Jews. But then Valkenberg proceeds to discuss the way people affiliated with the Gülen Movement often avoid explicit acknowledgments of their own Islam-inspired motivations. In empathetic mode, Valkenberg imagines some of the historical reasons for this including the intense vulnerabilities often experienced by religious people in the rigidly laicist history of Turkey. Nevertheless, among several other criticisms, he specifically challenges what seems to be an implicit assumption of Gülen-inspired interfaith efforts, namely that people must suppress their own religious identity in order to contribute to dialogue and integration. Such a posture, Valkenberg suggests, inevitably creates suspicion as witnessed in the common accusations that the Gülen movement has secret agendas and uses its organizations and "dialogue" events as ruses for Islamization. Valkenberg defends the Movement from these misguided caricatures while stating that they have nevertheless left themselves vulnerable to the charges. He then brings his essay full circle in an intriguing way by suggesting that Gülen needs to learn from Erasmus and contemporary Muslims such as Eboo Patel who show that you can only be a bridge-builder if you fully acknowledge your "specific point of departure." The moral: By owning their Islamic identity and motivations more clearly, Gülen followers will be better positioned to demonstrate their integrity and how their faith is compatible with modern values such as freedom and tolerance.

In chapter 8, Professor Paul Weller situates us in a very different corner of the early modern era by comparing what he calls the "Gülenian" Islamic vision for religious freedom with that of the "Baptistic" Christian vision that developed in 16th and 17th centuries. Weller finds "unusual clarity and consistency" in the Gülenian vision as well as many layers of overlap with the Baptistic vision. Both visions represent forces of notable influence for Islam and Christianity respectively, and both seek to represent and restore authentic forms of the respective faiths. Weller narrates the story of the development of Baptistic thought on religious freedom in the context of the struggles of 16th and 17th century Europe highlighting the remarkable vision of people like Thomas Helwys who, amidst high tensions and often violence, advocated not only for tolerance within his own Protestant communities but also for heretics, Turks, Jews and, most notably for the time, Catholics. Gülen's thought and influence, on the other hand, developed in the context of the post-Ottoman modern Turkish Republic in which he had to navigate the forces of, on the one hand, radical secularism and, on the other, both "obscurantist and oppositionist" forms of Islam. Weller weaves together a fascinating comparison noting, significantly, that both offer more than merely pragmatic or political visions that reflect modern contexts and ideas. Both, he says, are "profoundly theological," rooted in convictions about the nature and content of revealed truth. From such foundations, Weller finds both visions engaged in the quest for humble and fresh readings of scripture, both oppose the "reification" of specific traditions that threaten to undermine the integrity of their communities, and both seek a form of witness that navigates specific truth-claims while defending the freedom of others. Weller also notes the struggles of each to counter both theocratic tendencies in their wider communities as well as forms of pietistic withdrawal. In the end, Weller finds the Gülenian and Baptistic visions mutually committed to the importance of interfaith dialogue, an observation that can serve to challenge both the historical amnesia and the crass stereotypes that some project onto these communities today.

Chapters 9 contains the final essay which explores the religious worldviews and educational philosophies of The Gülen Movement and The Jesus Society (Jesuits). Beyond merely highlighting points of similarity, however, Fr. Patrick J. Howell presents hopeful invitations for more intentional collaboration. Howell starts by offering insights into the vastly different contexts that gave birth to these two movements. Discussing the founders, Howell remarks that Fethullah Gülen and Ignatius of Loyola "could not be more different." Ignatius was a Spanish Knight and priest who was born at the end of the 700-year *Reconquista* of the Christian Spanish Kingdom and was a primary leader in Catholic missionary efforts in response to the Protestant Reformation. Gülen is a Muslim cleric and preacher born in the post-Atatürk Republic of Turkey who, from the start, was especially interested in faithful and balanced responses to the rigid secularism which has been a part of Turkey since the early 20th century. Despite the distances of time, context, and experience, however, the essay locates substantial areas of overlap in the personal experiences and legacies of these two remarkable men. Of course, The Jesus Society (Jesuits) grew to become one of the most prominent Catholic orders in the world with its numerous initiatives for education, social justice, and dialogue. Similarly, Gülen is the inspiration for a huge and international network of activities and organizations often (and problematically) referred to as The Gülen Movement which especially focuses on education, philanthropy, and interfaith/intercultural bridge-building. Howell goes on to explore three salient religious features of each man's vision and practice. First, both were influenced by *mystical* streams of their religious traditions. Second, both placed great emphasis on pragmatic *action*. And finally, both were devoted to building *community*. In all this, Howell bridges the vastly different contexts of these religious leaders and movements providing opportunities for historical reflection and invitations to pragmatic collaboration.

John D. Barton
Pepperdine University
January 2017

List of Contributors

David B. Capes, PhD, is the Academic Dean of Houston Graduate School of Theology. He was the lead biblical scholar for The Voice Bible translation (Thomas Nelson, 2012). He has authored, co-authored, or co-edited many books, articles, book chapters, and reviews for scholarly and popular audiences, and spent twelve years as co-host of a local radio show called "A Show of Faith."

Fr. Patrick Howell SJ, a Jesuit priest, is a Distinguished Professor in the new Institute of Catholic Thought and Culture at Seattle University. For years, he wrote an inspirational religion column for the Seattle Times in conjunction with a Protestant pastor, a Jew, and a Muslim. He is the author of As Sure As the Dawn: A Spiritguide through Times of Darkness.

Özgür Koca, PhD, is an assistant professor of Islamic studies at Claremont School of Theology in California. His areas of expertise include Islamic philosophy, philosophies of science and religion, environmental ethics, contemporary Islamic movements, and interfaith dialogue. He is on the editorial boards of several scholarly journals including Science, Religion, and Culture and Journal of Dialogue Studies.

Fr. Thomas Michel, S.J. of Georgetown University is the former secretary of the Jesuit Secretariat for Interreligious Dialogue in Rome and former ecumenical secretary for the Federation of Asian Bishops' Conferences (1994-2008). Fr. Michel is a board member of Georgetown's Prince Alwaleed Bin Talal Center for Muslim-Christian Understanding, the Khalidi Library in Jerusalem, and the Journal of Islam and Muslim-Christian Relations.

Simon Robinson, PhD, is a professor of applied and professional ethics at Leeds Beckett University (UK), Faculty of Business and Law. He is the author of numerous books and papers on spirituality, ethics, leadership and management, and philosophy of responsibility.

Daniel W. Skubik, PhD, is a professor of law, ethics, and humanities at California Baptist University, Department of History and Government. He is the author of *At the Intersection of Legality and Morality: Hartian Law as Natural Law.*

Pim Valkenberg, PhD, is a professor of religion and culture at The Catholic University of America. His research interests include areas of theology, hermeneutics, and mysticism. His current projects include studies of Fethullah Gülen and the Hizmet movement and an interreligious reading of texts about the "Scripture People" in the Qur'an (co-authored).

Paul Weller, PhD, is Professor Emeritus of Inter-Religious Relations and Senior Research Fellow and Head of Research and Commercial Development, University of Derby (UK). He is also a research fellow in religion and society, Regents Park College, University of Oxford. He is the author, co-author, and editor of numerous publications and books, and is active in initiatives concerning religious dialogue and peace.

Salih Yücel, PhD, is an associate professor of Islamic studies at Charles Sturt University (Sydney, Australia). For ten years, he filled various ecclesiastical roles for the Ministry of Religious Affairs in Turkey. He also worked for seven years as a Muslim Chaplain at Harvard Medical School's hospitals and served for six years as senior lecturer at Centre for Religious Studies at Monash University.

PART ONE

GÜLEN AMONG CONTEMPORARY PEERS

CHAPTER ONE

FETHULLAH GÜLEN & ALASDAIR MACINTYRE: VIRTUE AND RELIGION IN MODERN LIFE

Daniel W. Skubik

> *Your true nature is even more virtuous than the angel's.*
> *The worlds are concealed in you. The universes are folded in you.*
> – Mehmet Akif (quoted in Sevindi 2008, 29)

Ethics Versus Virtue

Contemporary dominant discourses in ethics—East and West—for theorizing about how to realistically practice morality are grounded in the assessment of an action's measurable outcomes (consequentialism), its relation to the agent's duties and intentions (deontology), or its advancement/hindrance of ascribed rights (contractarianism). Among the more common derivative forms of these -isms and -ologies are utilitarianism (choose that course or rule of action which, all consequences considered, realizes the greatest happiness for the greatest number, with happiness meaning satisfaction of preferences or realization of pleasure and avoidance of pain); categorical imperatives (chose and perform selected actions out of duty to the commands of reason); and legalism (act as agreed to uphold the social contract founding the state to which one belongs).

It is periodically observed that these disparate discourses can still lead to similar proscriptions (e.g., the deliberate killing of an innocent human being is typically deemed wrongful by each), but they also too often prescribe opposing actions (e.g., a utilitarian might assert that lying in certain circumstances is morally preferable to truth-telling if the consequences of the former produce a better outcome than the latter, while a traditional Kantian will deny that lying is ever morally permissible, and a contractarian will ask whether the truth is formally owed by the speaker to the audience, and if not, the choice is an amoral, i.e. unregulated, one). In any event, assuming each discourse is internally coherent, their agreements and disagreements are not worth noting. It is simply a fact that they sometimes align and sometimes differ, and hence that people may disagree on what one ought to do or refrain from doing. Therefore, in light of there being no external, overarching principles or reasons that are universally agreed upon and that can be advanced to assert or deny the preferment of any one discourse over the others, the debate about what to do remains interminable between them. There can be no effective choice in adopting or eschewing any position on strictly rational grounds; one must simply elect as a matter of personal preference a particular moral stance.

These dominant discourses and interminable debates all focus principally on the action, the actor being merely a universalizable placeholder (anyone similarly situated should do or refrain from doing φ). However, there is another way of conceptualizing what one ought to do, which requires taking a step back, both in time and theory. I refer to a discourse dominant long ago, chiefly during the Axial Age (c. 800-200 BCE, as introduced by Karl Jaspers) that ran from Greece to North Africa, from India to China, though it has been shunted aside in modern times. It requires a focus on the virtues: on what sort of person one ought to be when acting, on the character of the particular actor who is acting in a specific context. It is commonly called virtue ethics.

Alasdair MacIntyre (1929 –) and Fethullah Gülen (1941 –) represent two voices that propose a return to virtue ethics in contemporary life. On the one hand, MacIntyre seeks to forge broad ties between a secular Aristotelian ethical theory and Judeo-Christian (most closely

Roman Catholic) religious ethics for purposes of realizing humanity's *telos* in today's confused and confusing post-Enlightenment world. On the other hand, Gülen can likewise be interpreted as seeking links between living a fully ethical and wholly faithful life in community with others who share those commitments by drawing on Sufi Islamic traditions of virtue in the context of religious devotion. This essay attempts to chart several of these key parallel developments in understanding virtue ethics in religious and communal contexts, and how they offer alternatives to the riven discourse so common today.

MacIntyre and Virtuous Persons

MacIntyre situates an understanding of the virtues within practices, which themselves are situated within a community living a certain sort of joined moral life. That is to say, virtues are not known or knowable abstractly, as essences or qualities in themselves or in persons who exhibit behaviors that might elicit commendation: truthfulness, justice, and courage are not Platonic ideals toward which we strive. Rather, to say something is a virtue is ordinarily to say that it is a disposition or settled pattern of behavior, "not only to act in particular ways, but also to feel in particular ways."[1] Further, since a virtue is intimately tied to practices, MacIntyre opines, "A virtue is an acquired human quality the possession and exercise of which tends to enable us to achieve those goods which are internal to practices and the lack of which effectively prevents us from achieving any such goods."[2] Accordingly, the virtue of truthfulness is not merely that one speaks the truth in a given setting, but that the particular speaker feels the appropriateness — even need — to speak the truth in the context of the relationships at stake in which the words are spoken. Further, truthfulness is a virtue of community import, and so of communal concern, to the extent that it is a disposition or settled pattern of behavior on the part of its members, enabling realization of the goods internal to the community's practices.

---

[1]   Alasdair MacIntyre, *After Virtue: A study in moral theory. 2nd ed.*, (Notre Dame: University of Notre Dame Press, 1984), 149.

[2]   MacIntyre, *After Virtue*, 191 [italics omitted]

This notion of practice is critical:

> By a "practice" I am going to mean any coherent and complex
> form of socially established cooperative human activity through
> which goods internal to that form of activity are realized in the
> course of trying to achieve those standards of excellence which
> are appropriate to, and partially definitive of, that form of activ-
> ity, with the result that human powers to achieve excellence,
> and human conceptions of the ends and good involved, are sys-
> tematically extended.[3]

As for internal and external goods (or what he later calls "goods of
excellence" and "goods of effectiveness"[4]), one should understand what
is gained from the practice that flows out from the practice itself, ver-
sus what is gained from participating in, but not because of, the practice.

This differentiation may seem strained, so consider an example
that MacIntyre uses to elucidate the point: Chess is a board game pursued in many countries around the world, but it is also a practice in the
strict sense outlined above. It is complex, and it requires cooperation to
have a fine play of the game. It has goods internal to it, such as development of all the players' analytical skills, strategic imaginations, and
competitive intensities; and it has goods external to it, such as prestige,
status, and money that winners can accrue.[5] The external goods are at
best circumstantially — rather than intimately or conceptually — tied
to the practice, and can be achieved without the virtues necessary to
attaining the internal goods of the practice. Internal goods can be realized only if the participants are committed to the practice for the sake
of the excellences that can be achieved therein as a feature of communal life, in that participants are related to each other in light of the rules
and excellences associated with the practice. One other important feature distinguishing internal from external goods is that the former

---

[3] MacIntyre, *After Virtue*, 187.

[4] Ted Clayton, "Political Philosophy of Alasdair MacIntyre," *The Internet Encyclopedia of Philosophy* (2005), http://www.iep.utm.edu/p-macint/ (last accessed September 2009), §6

[5] MacIntyre, *After Virtue*, 188.

comprises a positive-sum game while the latter returns a zero-sum game. In brief, external goods (say, cash winnings) become one participant's private property and thus one gains while others lose; internal goods (say, a striking endgame realized in a close match) can be enjoyed by and accepted as a benefit to all, not only the player. Virtues, then, are seen to be those dispositions or qualities that enable chess players to achieve goods internal to the practice, and without which internal goods could not be realized. Other practices follow this analytic pattern: engineering, farming, architecture, politics, even family life — all are practices with internal goods that help orient community members to each other, and provide the framework for a common life together.

Practices are many and varied, and the traditions or ways of life of the communities in which practices are situated are no less divergent. Therefore, we need something more to link virtues with practices in a community to avoid a dangerous indeterminacy that causes virtue to collapse on itself. We need to be able to understand and critique the varied existing conceptions of virtue. Just as "Aristotle's conception of justice and practical rationality articulated the claims of one particular type of practice-based community, ... Aquinas', like Ibn Roschd's or Maimonides', expressed the claims of a more complex form of community in which religious and secular elements coexist within an integrated whole."[6] In brief, all four sorts of communities can be said to follow virtue, but each of the four MacIntyre identifies here (classical Aristotelian, Roman Catholic/Thomistic, Islamic/Averroean and Jewish/Maimonidean) follow virtue in their own separate ways. They cannot be readily intermixed, intermingled, interwoven, or otherwise cross-lived, even when there are apparent points of perspectives and claims about the virtuous life that seem to be shared. That is because virtue is of a piece, and is never piecemeal; it forms an entire tapestry, not merely a widely shared design for threading.

---

6   Alasdair MacIntyre, *Whose Justice? Which Rationality?*, (Notre Dame: University of Notre Dame Press, 1988), 389.

Indeed, one must come to understand that there is a shared *telos* or purpose for all human beings, though the delineations of that *telos* will necessarily be differently sketched from one conception to another. As opposed to contemporary conceptions of political liberalism, which take pride in rejecting commitment to any particular conception of human good or the good life, a virtue ethicist of any sort must adopt one conception or another for virtue to have any purchase: "Absent any conception of what human beings are supposed to become if they realized their telos, there can be no ethical theory, because it simply has no purpose. For people with no destination, a road map has no value."[7] As further explicated by MacIntyre: "the best type of human life, that in which the tradition of the virtues is most adequately embodied, is lived by those engaged in constructing and sustaining forms of community directed towards the shared achievement of those common goods without which the ultimate human good cannot be achieved."[8] So where does one stand when there is no Archimedean external point for objective perspective on just what that *telos* or ultimate human good might be? For MacIntyre, that stance is Thomism: "When I wrote *After Virtue*, I was already an Aristotelian, but not yet a Thomist ... I became a Thomist after writing *After Virtue* in part because I became convinced that Aquinas was in some respects a better Aristotelian than Aristotle."[9] Metaphysics — one might interpolate a religiously-grounded metaphysics — hence cannot be avoided, indeed must be embraced, to complete a virtue ethics structure germane to human life situated in a community seeking the ultimate human good: "When we begin by asking what makes an action intelligible, we cannot avoid God."[10] Consequently, we might ourselves further extrapolate, atheist or agnostics can be

7   Clayton, "Political Philosophy of Alasdair MacIntyre," §10

8   Alasdair MacIntyre, *After Virtue: A Study in Moral Theory.* 3rd ed., (Notre Dame: University of Notre Dame Press, 2007), xiv

9   MacIntyre, *After Virtue 3rd ed.,* x

10   Stanley Hauerwas, "The Virtues of Alasdair MacIntyre," *First Things*, (October 2007). http://www.firstthings.com/article/2007/09/004-the-virtues-of-alasdair-macintyre-6 (last accessed September 2009)

ethical — at least in terms of the dominant ethical traditions previously outlined — but they can never be or become virtuous.

Gülen and Virtuous Persons

Gülen interestingly arrives at a quite similar destination, if by a different route. "The Islamic social system seeks to form a virtuous society ... virtues bring mutual support and solidarity."[11] This becomes abundantly clear in his discussion of the practices and virtues of Sufism. For example, the discussion of truthfulness (*sidq*) engages both individual and social development:

> Meaning true thoughts, true words and true actions, *sidq* is reflected in the life of a traveler on the path to God ... Truthfulness is the most reliable road leading to God, and the truthful are fortunate travelers upon it ... Truthfulness can be defined as struggling to preserve one's integrity and to avoid hypocrisy and lying, even in difficult circumstances when a lie will bring about salvation ... The way to true humanity lies in undertaking this grave responsibility.[12]

Thus, truthfulness is a matter of one's very being — a holistic concatenation of thought, word, and action, not simply a reflection of what one does or intends. Additionally, similar examples include discussions on straightforwardness (*istiqama*), patience (*sabr*), and modesty (*haya*). Each is grounded in Islam, with a focus on one's relationship to God and others, realized best in and through each practice/virtue presented.

However, also like MacIntyre, who grounds virtue in a particular religious tradition and metaphysics, Gülen does not demand conversion or adherence to such specifics, but rather to educate and dialogue on the basis of universals shared. As noted by Thomas Michel, General Secretary of the Vatican Secretariat for Interreligious Dialogue,

---

[11] Fethullah Gülen, *M.F. Gülen: Essays, Perspectives, Opinions*, (Compiled by The Fountain. Rutherford, NJ: The Light, Inc., 2002), 20.

[12] Fethullah Gülen, *Key Concepts in the Practice of Sufism: Emerald Hills of the Heart 1*, (Somerset, NJ: The Light, Inc., 2006), 84 & 88.

> When I asked about the surprising absence [in the "Gülen schools"] of what to me would have been an understandable part of a religiously inspired educational project, I was told that because of the pluralistic nature of the student bodies — Christian and Muslim in Zamboanga, and Buddhist and Hindu as well in Kyrghyzstan — that what they sought to communicate were universal values such as honesty, hard work, harmony, and conscientious service rather than any confessional instruction.[13]

Some of the specific virtues to be revealed or pursued include compassion and tolerance; hence, the "teacher is to be more than a lecturer or imparter of information. Rather, the teacher is an educator, one who reveals through his or her own self-presence who the student is to become."[14] Somewhat surprisingly, Gülen attends to vices as well, attempting to draw all that is human into the web of virtue:

> [T]here are human traits that seem to be evil at first glance, such as hatred, jealousy, enmity, the desire to dominate others, greed, rage, and egoism ... All human drives, needs, and desires, should be guided and trained in the direction of the eternal, universal, and invariable values that address the fundamental aspects of humanity ... All negative feelings can be transformed into sources of good by training and struggle.[15]

He expands on this latter point by noting, "People must be made to believe in goodness and beauty through a mild struggle against bad feelings and passions, not against other human beings."[16]

---

13 Gülen, *M.F. Gülen: Essays, Perspectives, Opinions*, 103
14 Barbara S. Boyd, "The Wisdom of Fethullah Gülen and the Truth of Parker Palmer: 'Enlightened Education as the Key to Global Transformation,'" *Proceedings of the Second International Conference on Islam in the Contemporary World: The Fethullah Gülen Movement in Thought and Practice*, (Norman: University of Oklahoma, 2006). http://fethullahgulenconference.org/ oklahoma/proceedings/BSBoyd.pdf (last accessed September 2009), 2.
15 Gülen, *M.F. Gülen: Essays, Perspectives, Opinions*, 25-26
16 Nevval Sevindi, *Contemporary Islamic Conversations: M. Fethullah Gülen on Turkey, Islam, and the West*, (Albany: State University of New York Press, 2008), 50.

Consequently, Gülen's conceptions of virtue and society are quite similar to MacIntyre's ideas of virtue and community: "Society is a collection of people who share similar feelings and ideas, who believe in similar things,"[17] though he is in fact leery of extending the power of the group over the individual and so tends to focus more on individual development of the virtues in one's own life. In this, Gülen is actually closer to classical Aristotle than is MacIntyre. Still, even if neither man is strictly speaking a communitarian in socio-political terms, both would agree with the observation that "to understand how values work, you must see them not as guiding us as individuals on our own but as guiding people who are trying to share their lives."[18] We are not alone, but always in relationship, never wholly acting only for ourselves, but always in connection to others.

MacIntyre, Gülen, and Virtuous Institutions

It is in this aspect of living in connection to others as propounded both by MacIntyre and Gülen that we can begin to develop an approach to an otherwise ticklish problem for virtue (and some other forms of) ethics: Can we reasonably speak of virtues of institutions? Are they even moral agents, amenable to these analyses of virtue? This is not, or at least not only, to bring up the metaphysical issue of whether formal institutions like corporations or highly organized social groups, like clubs, schools, religious denominations, or governments, are "beings" that can morally or legally be held accountable for their actions and thereby praised for their noble behavior and blamed for their defects. It is more a matter of determining what it might mean to say of an institution that it is the bearer of virtues (or vices) and that it does (or fails to) support the virtue-seeking community of which it is a functioning part. In short, it is to ask how we are to assess the value of institutional structures and operations if we are to take them seriously in a community where individu-

---

[17] Sevindi, *Contemporary Islamic Conversations*, 46
[18] Kwame Anthony Appiah. *Cosmopolitanism: Ethics in a World of Strangers* (NY: W.W. Norton & Co., 2006), 207.

als are themselves committed to a *telos*, leading to realization of ultimate human good.

We can begin by noting that institutions do embody their own practices, and those practices are embedded in a larger community in which realization of the excellences of those practices benefit both the actors within the institution as well as those in the broader community. Likewise, one can identify internal and external goods associated with those institutional practices, and can locate or identify virtues that both support and help expand the scope of the excellences at stake. To that extent then, our institutions look to be the carriers of practices that can inform the *telos* of the community, and so become amenable to further analysis.[19]

To carry through such an analysis, let's choose one particular form of institution important to today's world and construct a framework for understanding its role as an agent of virtue or vice in the relevant community. In today's global economy, corporations are institutions that are central to economic activity. More specifically, banks are corporations that are critical to local, national, and global economic activity, so can banks be agents of excellence in MacIntyre's and Gülen's senses? I think the answer is yes. Here's how:

Institutions are creators and bearers of practices that yield external goods. Banks are creators and bearers of practices that yield economic benefits to the communities they serve and profits to their corporate shareholders. It is an external good, for example, that a bank's practice of making commercial loans to only creditworthy customers yields a return on those investments while providing the capital necessary for productive economic activity by the debtor.

Banks are also participants in practices that bear internal goods, goods that can be realized only when the bank's employees pursue the excellences associated with the practices at issue. It is an internal good, for example, that a bank's commercial loan officers engage in the prac-

---

[19] Geoff Moore & Ron Beadle, "In Search of Organizational Virtue in Business: Agents, Goods, Practices, Institutions and Environments." *Organization Studies* 27, no.3 (2006): 369-389.

tice of establishing markers or rubrics to identify creditworthy customers so proper decisions can be made about whether and how much to consider loaning to an applicant. To do this requires honesty, straightforwardness, keen judgment, and investigative patience, which together will in turn allow expanding the critical scope of institutional operations for the benefit of the bank and of all the community members.

An institution needs, then, to construct a system of education and compliance measures that keeps these external and internal goods in balance. Consider the figure below, which comprises a single institutional matrix with dual indexes.

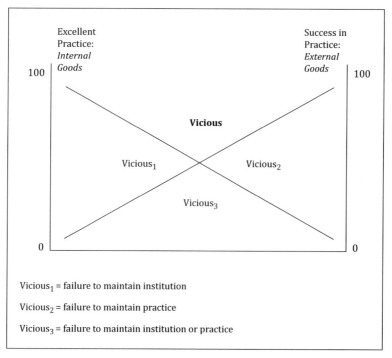

Figure 1. Institutional Matrix

Along the left side is the axis for indexing internal goods (0-100); on the right is the axis for indexing external goods (0-100). The curves represent the possible points for each index, with the quadrants of the matrix forming the spaces defining virtue and vice. Note that while there is only one space for virtuous banking activity — the space where internal and external goods are referenced above the curves' designated crossover point — there are three separate possible states of viciousness. The first form of vicious corporate banking is where the emphasis has fallen on maintaining internal goods, but there is no maintenance of external goods. That is, insufficient external goods will mean the dissolution of the bank as an institution, no matter the internal goods realized.

The second form of vicious corporate banking is where the emphasis has fallen on maintaining external goods, but there is no maintenance of internal goods. That is, insufficient internal goods will mean the failure of individuals working in or associated with the bank to develop personal virtue, and so the excellences associated with those practices will dissipate, resulting in the disappearance of the practices themselves along with their associated virtues.

The third form of vicious corporate banking is where the emphasis has been insufficient to maintain either internal or external goods, and so both the institution and the practices will disappear.

What does this mean in a real world setting? I think a fair and interesting interpretation of our current financial straits are a function of the second form of viciousness: So much energy and effort was devoted to achieving external goods (like the explosion of the CDS market) that practices critical to sustaining virtues and excellences withered and disappeared. The third form of viciousness is representative of small and even medium-sized local and regional banks that have recently failed and been taken over by the FDIC because they could not sustain either external or internal goods. I am not aware of any real-world examples of the first form of viciousness, but one that might possibly fit comes to mind from the movies: The small building-and-loan operation in Frank Capra's celebrated 1946 film, *It's a Wonderful Life*, portrays George Bailey (Jimmy Stewart) as the bank's manager, facing financial failure and criminal indictment for a shortage on the books not entirely of his own making.

More apposite, I suppose, is whether we have any examples of virtuous banking. I think we do, especially in the many relatively small credit unions around the U.S. that have done quite well even in these difficult times. Further, I think we can see the important development of such examples in the growing Islamic banking sector around the world. Islamic banking seeks to develop alternatives to interest-bearing financial instruments and the expansion of debt markets with which we are otherwise familiar in the West. In particular, such banks are created not simply to fill a niche in the global marketplace, but rather, the shariah-compliant option was "intended to help in the formation of the 'Islamic personality.' In this way through the sum of their individual transactions, Muslims would create the basis for an Islamic economy. It was to be a case of private virtue leading to public virtue."[20] To the extent that there is serious commitment to developing an institution that embodies both practices for excellence and success in external goods, we have the makings of a virtuous institution that contributes appropriately to the community of which it is a part. An interesting example of such a virtuous-minded, middle-way forward in banking in Islamic terms is found in Bank Asya (Asya Finans Kurumu AŞ), a Turkish banking organization (along with its insurance subsidiary, Işik Sigorta) that is associated with Gülen and his followers.[21] It provides a mix of transactional accounts — some of which are standard interest-bearing monetary vehicles, while others are non-interest-bearing and shariah-compliant — to meet the needs of a variety of retail and commercial clients, as it operates under the secular Turkish state umbrella. Thus, while the state perforce takes no position on particular forms of ethics or virtue theories (its concern, as for any secular state, is legality, or adherence to civil mandates), the banking institution itself is free to operate in legal and chosen ethical or virtuous fashion.

[20] Charles Tripp, *Islam and the Moral Economy: The Challenge of Capitalism*, (Cambridge: Cambridge University Press, 2006), 135.

[21] Filiz Başkan, "The Political Economy of Islamic Finance in Turkey: The Role of Fethullah Gülen and Asya Finans," *The Politics of Islamic Finance*, (Edinburgh: Edinburgh University Press, 2004), 224-226 & 236; and Daniel Skubik, "Fethullah Gülen, Islamic Banking and Global Finance," *A Survey of International Corporate Responsibility*, 289-304, (Charlottesville, VA: Philosophy Documentation Center, 2009).

If this analysis is overall sound, then it applies equally well to other institutions of community life, such as synagogues, churches, mosques, and temples, as well as schools and universities, civic clubs and small businesses, and so forth. That is, each religious or other social institution is necessarily a generator and carrier of internal goods within its community, even while it lives out a mission dedicated in part to realization of external goods for its continuing life and success. Its place in the community is affirmed to the extent it successfully meets both sets of community needs for internal as well as external goods, which together help realize the community's vision of the *telos*. In short, only when institutions are virtuous will the virtue of the people be able to flourish. Individuals cannot thrive alone.

Conclusion

Of course, one needs more than a common rhetoric or hope of practice. If unfussy acquiescence to modern pluralism reduces talk of virtue to the lowest common denominator, then like a secular or civic religion, we will have the outward form without any inward substance. As MacIntyre has warned: "What the morality of the virtues articulated in and defended by the moral rhetoric of our political culture provides is, it turns out, not an education in the virtues, but, rather, an education in how to seem virtuous, without actually being so."[22] If we are to realize and find refuge in true virtue, whether as individuals, as families, as small groups, or as institutions of social significance, we must together do so in deliberate and deliberately chosen communities of faith.

Works Cited

Appiah, Kwame Anthony. *Cosmopolitanism: Ethics in a World of Strangers.* NY: W.W. Norton & Co., 2006.

Başkan, Filiz. "The Political Economy of Islamic Finance in Turkey: The Role of Fethullah Gülen and Asya Finans." C.M. Henry and R. Wilson (eds.). *The Politics of Islamic Finance.* Edinburgh: Edinburgh University Press, (2004): 216-239.

---

[22] MacIntyre, "How to Seem Virtuous Without Actually Being So," 131

Boyd, Barbara S. "The Wisdom of Fethullah Gülen and the Truth of Parker Palmer: 'Enlightened Education as the Key to Global Transformation.'" *Proceedings of the Second International Conference on Islam in the Contemporary World: The Fethullah Gülen Movement in Thought and Practice.* Norman: University of Oklahoma, 2006. http://fethullahgulenconference.org/oklahoma/proceedings/BSBoyd.pdf (last accessed September 2009).

Clayton, Ted. "Political Philosophy of Alasdair MacIntyre." *The Internet Encyclopedia of Philosophy*, 2005. http://www.iep.utm.edu/p-macint/ (last accessed September 2009).

Gülen, M. Fethullah. *M.F. Gülen: Essays, Perspectives, Opinions.* Compiled by The Fountain. Rutherford, NJ: The Light, Inc., 2002.

Gülen, M. Fethullah. *Key Concepts in the Practice of Sufism: Emerald Hills of the Heart 1.* Translated by Ali Ünal. Somerset, NJ: The Light, Inc., 2006.

Hauerwas, Stanley. "The Virtues of Alasdair MacIntyre." *First Things*, 2007. http://www.firstthings.com/article/2007/09/004-the-virtues-of-alasdair-macintyre-6 (last accessed September 2009).

MacIntyre, Alasdair. *After Virtue: A Study in Moral Theory.* 2nd ed. Notre Dame: University of Notre Dame Press, 1984.

MacIntyre, Alasdair. *Whose Justice? Which Rationality?* Notre Dame: University of Notre Dame Press, 1988.

MacIntyre, Alasdair. "How to Seem Virtuous Without Actually Being So." *Education in Morality.* Edited by M. Halstead and T. McLaughlin. London: Routledge, (1999): 118-131.

MacIntyre, Alasdair. *After Virtue: A study in moral theory.* 3rd ed. Notre Dame: University of Notre Dame Press, 2007.

Moore, Geoff, and Ron Beadle. "In Search of Organizational Virtue in Business: Agents, Goods, Practices, Institutions and Environments." *Organization Studies* 27, no. 3 (2006): 369-389.

Sevindi, Nevval. *Contemporary Islamic Conversations: M. Fethullah Gülen on Turkey, Islam, and the West.* Edited with Introduction by Ibrahim M. Abu-Rabi'. Translated by Abdullah T. Antepli. Albany: State University of New York Press, 2008.

Skubik, Daniel. "Fethullah Gülen, Islamic Banking and Global Finance." In J. Hooker, J. Hulpke, & P. Madsen (eds). *A Survey of International Corporate Responsibility.* Charlottesville, VA: Philosophy Documentation Center, (2009): 289-304.

Tripp, Charles. *Islam and the Moral Economy: The Challenge of Capitalism.* Cambridge: Cambridge University Press, 2006.

CHAPTER TWO

THE SPIRITUALITY OF PEACEBUILDING: FETHULLAH GÜLEN AND JOHN PAUL LEDERACH

Simon Robinson

Introduction

Both Fethullah Gülen and John Paul Lederach are focused on the practice of peacebuilding; but the definition of this term needs clarifying. Some argue that it involves the period of post-conflict reformation, when peace is to be built and sustained, and reconciliation established.[1] Neither Gülen nor Lederach easily fit into that definition. For his part, Lederach does formally practice peacebuilding in the post-conflict phase (including work in Somalia, Nicaragua and Northern Ireland), but much like George Mitchell, he recognizes that the skills of peacebuilding are often in play well before the conflict has ceased.[2] It is part of the commitment to the process of listening and building trust that leads to the cessation of conflict in the first place. In all this, Lederach recognizes that peacebuilding is less about techniques and more about ontology — the very being of the person and the social and envi-

---

[1] Boutros Boutros-Ghali, *An Agenda for Peace Preventive diplomacy, peacemaking and peace-keeping*, (1992): http://www.un.org/en/peace building/pbso/pbun. shtml.

[2] *George Mitchell, Making Peace: The Inside Story of the Making of the Good Friday Agreement*, (London: Heinemann, *1999).*

ronmental networks of which he or she is a part. Lederach is a committed Mennonite Christian, but the spirituality of his peacebuilding is not based in theology so much as a broad generic spirituality, outlined in his book *The Moral Imagination*.[3]

Gülen's approach to peacebuilding is less explicit. The *Hizmet* Movement (founded, though not led, by him) does not claim a formal peacebuilding role, but is nonetheless informed by his views on peacebuilding. It is also more firmly based in theology and the role of humanity in relation to creation. For him, peacebuilding is part of a response to God and is evidenced in the development of key institutions and relationships which enable the right response to God and His creation. From that theological position, he moves to a broader spirituality focused in human relationships which is quite complementary to Lederach.

In both cases, Gülen and Lederach span the divide between sacred and secular because of their focus on the network or web of social and physical environments, and the responsibility of humanity to respond and create. This reveals a spirituality that is genuinely holistic, based in tolerance and care, focused in action, and tempered by rationality.

The Gülen Movement and Peacebuilding

Esposito and Yilmaz suggest that Gülen's view of peacebuilding is based in a proactive stance, involving optimism.[4] However, I want to suggest instead the term hope. There are many attempts to define optimism, not least in relation to hope, with both seen as a positive emotion.[5] Elsewhere I have suggested a clear distinction between optimism as a generalized positive attitude to the future, and hope as a virtue involving the capacity to envision the future in a positive way.[6] Hope as

---

3   John Paul Lederach, *The Moral Imagination*, (Oxford: Oxford University Press, 2005).

4   John Esposito and Ihsan Yilmaz eds., *Islam and Peacebuilding: Gülen Movement Initiatives*, (New York: Blue Dome, 2010).

5   Patricia Bruininks and Bertram Malle, "Distinguishing Hope from Optimism and Related Affective States," *Motivation and Emotion*, 29, no. 4 (2005): 327-355.

6   Simon Robinson, *Spirituality, Ethics and Care*, (Joanna Kingsley: London, 2008).

a virtue suggests that this is a disposition that can be practiced and developed. Snyder argues that this is related to action, the capacity to make things happen, and as such, is based in clear goals, agency, awareness and development of pathways.[7] This coincides with Gülen's view of peacebuilding because it connects the virtue of hope to the core idea of *hizmet* (active service). We are able to envision the particular future in terms of clear goals, we take responsibility for pursuing those goals (developing agency), and we can see clear pathways to achieving those goals. Such a view of hope provides a framework for considering Gülen's peacebuilding.

Taking each of those aspects of hope, we first see that Gülen is focused in core morally significant goals, not least of which is service (*hizmet*), which is focused in a response to God and taking responsibility for His creation. Humanity thus takes on the role of vicegerent.[8] The created world embodies difference and plurality. Hence, Gülen is less concerned about providing exact equality of outcome or resources, and more about response to the particularity and particular needs in the social and physical environment. Nonetheless, in social terms, he notes three significant factors that are necessary to engage these environments: knowledge, material resources, and unity of purpose and action. Conversely, Gülen then has three giants that he aims to slay:[9] ignorance, poverty, and disunity.[10] Unlike the giants of Beveridge this goes beyond attempts to address deficits (of knowledge and material resources) and notes the underlying problem of disunity. At one level, this seems to accept that disunity, and thus potential conflict, is part of

---

[7] C.R. Synder, "The past and possible futures of hope," *Journal of Social and Clinical Psychology* 19, no. 1 (Spring 2000): 11-28.

[8] Fethullah Gülen, *Towards a Global Civilization of Love and Tolerance*, (New Jersey: The Light, 2004): 122.

[9] The term giant is no longer used by Gülen but comes from William Beveridge's plans (1943) for the Welfare State in the UK: squalor, ignorance, want, idleness, disease. See Nicholas Timmins, *The Five Giants: A Biography of the Welfare State*, (London: Harper Collins, 2001).

[10] Mustafa Gürbüz, "Performing Moral Opposition: Musings on the Strategy and Identity in the Gülen Movement," *Muslim World in Transition:Contributions of the Gülen Movement,* (London: Leeds Metropolitan University Press 2007): 104-117.

the fabric of the social environment. In light of that, peacebuilding becomes central to any service, and addressing these giants then forms the basis of some clear goals involving education, development, and dialogue.

Education and Development

The pathways to achieving core goals are clearly worked out by Gülen. First, ignorance has to be addressed by the development of education. Education, for Gülen, is based in the development of character, which focuses on continual self-criticism and self-renewal. Such self-examination "enables the believer to make amends for past mistakes and be absolved in the sight of God, for it provides a constant realization of the self-renewal in one's inner world."[11] At its heart, therefore, are core peace virtues of renewal and reconciliation with the self and others. This character-development involves, in effect, the development of responsibility for one's own thinking and underlying values and how these are embodied in practice.[12] This involves modelling values and virtues in practice in the school community and culture, as well as drawing in families, and thus connecting different aspects of the students' lives. This is not prescriptive but focused precisely in the development of responsive agency. Hence, Gülen espouses a form of freedom.[13] This freedom involves neither the negative (freedom from) or positive (freedom to) freedom noted by Berlin,[14] but rather a freedom closer to Aquinas, exemplified in Novak.[15] This stresses self-mastery and ordering the passions, developing autonomy and agency through reflective deliberative decision-making. Agency is precisely gained

---

[11] Fethullah Gülen, *Key Concepts in the Practice of Sufism* 1, (Fairfax: The Fountain, 1999).

[12] Fethullah Gülen, *Essays, Perspectives, Opinions* 2nd ed., (Somerset, N.J.: The Light, 2006): 16.

[13] Gülen, *Essays, Perspectives, Opinions*

[14] Isaiah Berlin, "Two Concept of Liberty," A. Quinton ed., *Political Philosophy*, (Oxford: Oxford University Press, 1969): 141-153.

[15] Michael Novak, *Morality, Capitalism and Democracy*, (London: IEA, 1990).

through the development of the virtues that underlie these activities.[16] Like Novak, Gülen sees the exercise of personal responsibility as then leading to broader social responsibility, involving better distribution of resources and more cooperation for social ends. A good example of this is the way that businessmen of the *Hizmet* Movement work together to provide resources to the Gülen schools.[17]

The founding of these schools, then, provides a clear pathway, enabling a response to ignorance and the development of human agency. Hence, Gülen schools are centered in science, language skills, and educational excellence (not in ideology or prescription, educational or religious), enabling the development of people who can take responsible leadership roles in business and society. In all this, it becomes possible for Islam to take its place in a post-modern age as key for the development of society. As Ünal and Williams put it, "[e]ducation through learning and a commendable way of life is a sublime duty that manifests the Divine Name *Rabb* (Upbringer and Sustainer). By fulfilling it, we attain the rank of true humanity and become a beneficial element to society."[18]

The response to that society is made more effective the more that responsibility is shared. In turn, this generates further hope through opening up multiple transparent pathways, widening possibilities through negotiation of responsibilities.[19]

Education at its root is about the dynamics of peace, enabling the development and sharing of responsibility for the self and for the social and physical environment. At its heart is consciousness and appreciation of the other as human, including the capacity to challenge as well as support. While this provides general peace pathways, there are good

---

16 Novak, *Morality, Capitalism and Democracy*, 16
17 Yasien Mohamed, "The Ethical Theory of Fethullah Gulen and its Practice in South Africa," *The Muslim World In Transition*, (London: Leeds Metropolitan University Press, 2007).
18 Ali Ünal, and Alphonse Williams, *Advocate of Dialogue: Fethullah Gulen*, (Fairfax, Virginia: Fountain, 2009): 308.
19 Andrew Lester, *Hope in Pastoral Care and Counselling*, (Louisville: John Knox Press, 1995).

examples of direct involvement in pre- and post-conflict situations in which the schools provide particular realistic hope. These include establishing schools open to children from all sides in areas of conflict, including the Balkans, Northern Iraq, Northern Ireland, and the Philippines.[20] A good example is the school in Skopje, Macedonia where children from across the divide were being educated while their parents were at war.[21] This generates a situation analogous to Lederach's web watching and connecting (see below), in which actors from all sides can begin to see where they all connect to the social web and are thus part of that web, in this case through a shared concern for children. This is further reinforced by education at all levels including university,[22] and on plurality in education itself, not least in terms of gender inclusivity.[23] This is also reflected in the *Hizmet* Movement's work in Kenya and Uganda. Core to this has been a focus on the use of local resources, rather than international aid,[24] including educating women and stressing the roles of women in education and wider society. As Yilmz and Esposito note, studies have suggested that where women are empowered in social, economic, and political terms, societies are less likely to become involved in conflict.[25]

In all of this there is also a connection to poverty alleviation, partly through an educational focus in areas such as Kyrgyzstan, implicitly

---

[20] Zeki Sarıtoprak, "Fethullah Gülen's Theology of Peacebuilding," *Islam and Peacebuilding: Gülen Movement Initiatives*, (New York: Blue Dome 2010).

[21] Saritopra, "Fethullah Gülen's Theology of Peacebuilding," 637

[22] Talip Küçükcan, "Social and Spiritual Capital of the Gülen Movement," *Muslim World in Transition: Contributions of the Gülen Movement*, (London: Leeds Metropolitan University Press 2007): 187.

[23] Robert Hefner, "Introduction: Modernity and the Remaking of Muslim Politics," *Remaking Muslim Politics: Pluralism, Contestation, Democratization*, (Princeton: Princeton University Press, 2005): 27.

[24] Mehmet Kalyoncu, "Gülen-inspired Schools in the East Africa: Secular Alternative in Kenya and Pragmatist Approach to Development in Uganda," *Islam in the Age of Global Challenges: Alternative Perspectives of the Gülen Movement Conference Proceedings*, (Washington DC: Rumi Forum 2008): 350.

[25] John Esposito and Ihsan Yilmaz eds., *Islam and Peacebuilding: Gülen Movement Initiatives*, New York: Blue Dome, 2010.

linking economics to peace building,[26] partly though business investment in such areas and partly through the development of poverty relief and humanitarian aid charity organizations such as *Kimse Yok Mu?*[27]

Dialogue

If internal or external disunity is the third major giant, then dialogue, tolerance and mutual understanding are the remedies.[28] These interconnect with the development of agency.

At the heart of the Gülen philosophy and action is dialogue. His stress on spirituality, rationality, and action in the public realm inevitably takes this dialogue out of a narrow range of interfaith dialogue to inter-cultural dialogue. This has led to many different groups — such as the Intercultural Dialogue Centre[29] and the Dialogue Society in London[30] — and the development of dialogue platforms, not least the Abant Platform of the Journalists and Writers Foundation. These efforts have brought together intellectuals, activists, journalists, and leaders of different groups. In 2007, the Abant Platform developed intra-faith dialogue in Turkey between the Sunni and the Alevi minority. As Küng suggests, inter- and intra-faith dialogue is key to wider peace building, "There will be no peace among the nations without peace among the religions. There will be no peace among the religions without dialogue among the religions."[31]

Dialogue to Gülen is key to peacebuilding focused in education, enabling the practice of dialogue in the community of learning practice, and also in examples such as media outlets developed by the *Hizmet*

---

[26] Mitchell (1999) links economics to sustainable post-conflict development in the Northern Ireland peace project.

[27] Thomas Michel, "Fighting Poverty with Kimse Yok Mu?" *Islam in the Age of Global Challenges: Alternative Perspectives of the Gülen Movement Conference Proceedings,* Washington DC: Rumi Forum (2008): 350-373.

[28] Esposito and Yilmaz, *Islam and Peacebuilding*

[29] http://www.gyv.org.tr

[30] http://www.dialoguesociety.org/

[31] Donald Musser, and Dixon Sunderland, *War or Words: Interreligious Dialogue as an Instrument of Peace*, (Cleveland: The Pilgrim Press 2005): 1.

Movement. Dialogue is central to all the thought and action noted above, focusing on three interconnected aspects: consciousness of creation and the call to care for it, giving an account of thought and action, and creative action. In the first of these, dialogue is critical to the development of consciousness of the environment and its nature in relation to God. Dialogue further enhances relationships with the other, who shares responsibility for that environment. In one respect it reveals the sameness of the other, something focused on in the interfaith dialogue platforms and through stress on universal values. It also focuses on difference, and with that the importance of tolerance, again central to Gülen's thinking. As Pratt notes, tolerance for Gülen is not passive acceptance but involves proactive engagement with the other — both seeing the other as part of humanity and as a potential co-creator.[32]

Such dialogue enables the development of a realistic and truthful assessment of the data in any situation, and the development of agency. It demands articulation of value and practice, which clarifies both what we think and do. Dialogue itself, though, also develops critical thinking. Even just the different perspective of the other questions and sharpens one's own values and core concepts. This dialogue becomes even richer in the light of Gülen's holism, synoptic thinking and plural identity; the dialogue is not simply around ideas, and with that the danger of moving into the defense of ideas. Huntington's thesis of the clash of civilizations — that post-Cold War conflict will be focused in religious or cultural identities — is precisely located there.[33] A holistic perspective, however, involves getting to know the self and other in relation to mutual plural culture, involving feelings and ideas, all focused in responsive action. This involves mutual challenge and mutual learning, with an output not of defense but action. This is what pleases God, not defending right thinking. Hence, such dialogue primarily involves genuine engagement with the other, as person, project, or place, and not

[32] Douglas Pratt, "Islamic Prospects for Interreligious Dialogue: The Voice of Fethullah Gülen," *Islam and Peacebuilding: Gülen Movement Initiatives*, (New York: Blue Dome, 2010): 189-206.

[33] Samuel Huntington, *The Clash of Civilizations and the Remaking of World Order*, (New York: Touchstone, 1998).

the assertion of the organization's location or identity in the public realm. All of these elements demand that this involves not simply being responsible for critical thinking but also for the feelings that emerge around any felt sense of identity or core values.

Dialogue can be seen as the key means of advancing accountability. In one sense, this involves dialogue as the major means of producing transparency. Writers such as Park suggest that the *Hizmet* Movement is not institutionally transparent.[34] In one sense, this is true. With many different groups involved in the movement, it is difficult to see how accountability can be worked through in a simple or linear way. However, the dynamic nature of dialogue itself embodies transparency, precisely because it requires all parties to give an account of their meaning and practice, and thus be held accountable for it. In many of the conferences organized by the *Hizmet* Movement over the last decade, this has involved openness to critiques from different perspectives, not least in dialogue, around the role of women in and the governance of the movement.[35]

Such transparency enables the movement to give an account to society in general, and this is an important development of dialogue beyond simple bilateral relationships. This is not a free-flow of meaning between participants, such as Bohm's theory of dialogue.[36] Rather, the dialogue is focused in shared accountability to God and the global environment, and with that, accountability to many different stakeholders, from the state to religion to other nations. This multiple accountability, which has echoes of Mikhail Bakhtin's[37] focus on the interplay of many different voices, demands an awareness of the different stakeholders, and is held together by the stress on *hizmet*. There

---

[34] William Park, "The Fethullah Gulen Movement," *The Middle Eastern Review of International Affairs* 12, no 3 (2008): 1-11.

[35] Helen Rose Ebaugh, *The Gülen Movement: A Sociological Analysis of a Civic Movement Rooted in Moderate Islam*, (London: Springer, 2009).

[36] David Bohm, *On Dialogue*, (London: Routledge, 1996).

[37] Mikhail Bakhtin, *Problems of Dostoevsky's Poetics*, (Minneapolis, MN: University of Minnesota, 1929).

are also echoes of Friere's view of dialogue (as non- directive) in the way that leadership is dispersed in the movement.[38]

Dialogue also demands the development of commitment to the self and the other.[39] It is not possible to pursue dialogue without giving space and time for it to develop, and this in turn demands a non-judgemental attitude. Commitment to the self and others is also essential if the potential critique of values and practice is to emerge from articulation and reflection. The practice of dialogue also enables listening, and with that, empathy, appreciation and responsiveness. We learn about the other as well as ourselves only if we are open to both. This deepens any sense of accountability to the other in the dialogue.

In the third part of dialogue the stress is on action. Gülen suggests that we do not have to reach absolute agreement before working through the shared social issues, such as ignorance, poverty, and discrimination.[40] On the contrary, these provide a shared area of concern and, along with the shared values, can be worked through regardless of differences. The stress on action strengthens the holistic framework. Action tests the accountability and commitment of those involved in the dialogue. Being accountable for actions also involves testing the actions against purpose and meaning. The actions themselves then become the basis for reflection on meaning. Such reflection then becomes the basis for the development of integrity, connecting the different voices and practice.

Such a dynamic state also enables the development of shared responsibility, not simply the recognition of shared interests. It leads to the negotiation of responsibility, exemplified in the way that businesses develop decisions around funding the work of the movement. This is very different from Habermas' view of dialogue based primarily in

---

[38] Paulo Friere, *Pedagogy of the Oppressed*, (New York: Continuum, 1972).

[39] Michael Graskemper, "A Bridge to Interreligious Cooperation: The Gülen-Jesuits Educational Nexus," *Muslim World in Transition: Contributions of the Gülen Movement*, (London: Leeds Metropolitan University Press 2007): 622-631.

[40] Fethullah Gülen, "Sorumluluk Suuru," *Yeni Ümit Magazine*, (July-September 1995): 29.

developing conceptual consensus.[41] The effect of working through shared responsibility is to extend the imagination and develop creativity. It shows what is possible, especially where responsibility is shared, and so increases the capacity to respond. In all this, dialogue both develops the responsibility at the heart of Gülen's thinking and directly enables the agency, goals, and pathways of hope. Because it is relation-centered, it includes forgiveness and reconciliation.[42] Grinell suggests that all of this makes it easy for Gülen to be a "boarder transgressor," to operate beyond boundaries.[43] I would argue, however, that the idea of transgression does not easily fit the dynamic of dialogue or responsibility. Gülen's stress on plurality, dialogue and responsibility,[44] rather, points to a sense of multiple responsibility built around the person's relationships with different areas in the social environment. In this sense, the person has responsibilities that transcend different boundaries. Bridges across those boundaries are then based in the capacity of the person or group to inhabit the different areas, and to generate dialogue with the different narratives and narrators.

Media

The media outlets of the *Hizmet* Movement give a good example of how dialogue is enabled in practice. The outlets include television channels, publishing outlets, and newspapers. Behind many of these projects is the Writers and Journalists Foundation. *Zaman Daily* is a prime example of a newspaper. It offers both a focus of dialogue and, perhaps more importantly, the conditions for dialogue. Kerim Balci has suggested that there are five key principles embodied in the *Zaman Media* group.[45] The

---

[41] Jürgen Habermas, *The Theory of Communicative Action,* (Boston: Beacon Press, 1984).

[42] Pratt, "Islamic Prospects for Interreligious Dialogue: The Voice of Fethullah Gülen"

[43] Klas Grinell, "Border Thinking: Fethullah Gulen and the East West Divide," *Islam and Peacebuilding: Gülen Movement Initiatives*, (New York: Blue Dome 2010): 65-84.

[44] Simon Robinson, "Islam Responsibility and Business," *Islam In the West*, (Basingstoke: Plagrave 2012): 154-168.

[45] I am grateful to Kerim Balci, formerly of the Turkish Review and now at the Zaman, who shared these with me on a research trip to Istanbul in May 2013.

principles are not a written code of conduct, but are focused in the practice. These are:

1. Good news is also good news
2. No sensationalism
3. No denigration, no defamation
4. Text-intensivity
5. Being in equal closeness to all political parties

Strikingly, these are not peacebuilding principles per se. However, they provide a context for peacebuilding, which recognizes that it is the responsibility of journalism to enable ongoing dialogue. The first principle is partly focused in the Turkish context where the press had practiced mainly pejorative journalism, reflecting a negative, pessimistic view of human nature, society, and the state and God. This demands a clear awareness of the social and physical environment and therefore, an appreciation of the positive aspects of creation — sharing the good news as well as the bad.

The second principle refines the first, noting that sensationalist journalism tends to focus not on data and information so much as entertaining the reader, often through the pain of others. Hence, if there is news of violence, it should be accompanied by analysis and possible solutions. Both of these principles have their roots in Sufi tradition. Not only is the universe created in the best possible way,[46] but depiction of the world should also be in a good way. Sufis believe that an event and its story are two distinct events, each with distinct moral value, not least because the depiction can affect responses to the story.

By 2001, it was decided to find criteria of measuring how well the story was told. This led, for example, to the use of full verbal sentences in headlines so they were not ambiguous, and avoiding large character headlines that imply sensation. If the headline in itself is not enough to clearly state the content of the news item, then use is made of extra spot lines to rapidly explain to the reader the content of the article.

---

[46] There are echoes here of Leibniz and subsequently the Great Chain of Being; see Lovejoy, *The Great Chain of Being*.

The third principle is partly about ensuring no denigration of groups or individuals, but also about ensuring that the voices of different ethnic groups, religious groups, and other groups are heard in the paper (through hiring diverse columnists). Again this reflects the importance of hearing different narratives and how they relate to the story. Again, while the paper does not specifically relate this to peacemaking, the connection is clear. The effect is to hold together narrative, narrator, and events. In other words, journalism begins to move beyond simply reporting events to an awareness and appreciation of different narratives and the narrators themselves, and how they relate the story and the wider environments. In other words, it begins to affect the perception of the other, both as part of the same environment and as part of the dialogue about the environment, an idea to which we will return in Lederach below.

The fourth principle begins to focus further on the means of communication. *Zaman* is text intensive. This means more space for lengthy, analytical pieces often supplied by academics and thus setting up more different perspectives. More text needs more time for the readers to engage with the discourse. This in turn leads to the development of a stabilized readership (further committed through subscription), which begins also to contribute to the debate. *Zaman* also uses a high Turkish in the search for a richer vocabulary and more rigorous articulation of ideas.

The final principle is of political disinterestedness in the sense of equal distance from all political parties. This does not preclude taking views of political policies, not least support for transparent governance, democracy, minority rights, and responsible capitalism. Key to this stance is the capacity to challenge all parties and interests, in both political and civil society,[47] and thus encourages output from all levels of society.

In short then, the media is a good example of Gülen's dialogue focus in practice, providing a framework for dialogue and supporting mutual responsibility, which is central to peacebuilding. This builds a practice

---

[47] Extending, for instance, to dialogue about Gülen's critique of the Gaza flotilla.

that transcends interest or ideology. In effect, this is the practice of practical wisdom (*phronesis*), reflection on the good of any practice, focused in dialogue. There is about this something of an ongoing learning dynamic, focused in *ijtihad*, the idea of continuous interpretation in a "proper intellectual and spiritual struggle."[48] In all this, Gülen and the *Hizmet* Movement do not claim the formal title of peacebuilders, but see this as running throughout their practice, bridging individualism and communitarianism.

Lederach, Difference, and Peacebuilding

There are many echoes of Gülen once we turn to J.P. Lederach. Neither are systematic theologians, but both have a strong sense of spirituality and the capacity to articulate that in the public sphere,[49] and both are concerned with a holistic approach to peacebuilding and focus on the virtues needed to develop peacebuilding. For Lederach, however, there is a very different feel to the theory and practice of peacebuilding. Lederach is less concerned about clear pathways and more concerned with character that enables an on-going, flexible response. The key image is of the journey, and of a response to that journey that is more about the practice of an art than the development of scientific thinking. This is less about confidence in core goals and pathways and more about the capacity to manage uncertainty. Hence, the holism that he espouses is more focused in feeling, empathy, and interpretation.

Conflict and Transformation

Lederach builds on Ricoeur, recognizing that identity, and with that, perception, is constructed.[50] Conflict is, "among other things, the process of building and sustaining very different perceptions and interpre-

---

48 Pratt, "Islamic Prospects for Interreligious Dialogue: The Voice of Fethullah Gülen," 200

49 Lederach has a Mennonite background.

50 Paul Ricoeour, *Onself as Another*, (Chicago: Chicago University Press, 1992).

tations of reality."[51] This means that conflict is based in personal and cultural dynamics, often focused on sustaining difference.

Difference is often associated with division and, subsequently, conflict. Such difference, expressed in different narratives and interests within organizations and beyond, is an inevitable part of the social and physical environment. Peacebuilding approaches, most often linked with major conflict, can also be used in engaging difference before the advent of conflict. Lederach suggests that dynamics that sustain the polarized view of the world are largely emotional and defensive. In the worst cases, this leads to cycles of conflict in which the perception, and related values and worldview, is reinforced by the response of the other. It is thus important to address the perception of difference and the underlying emotional narrative that has emerged, leading to the possibility of transformation. For Lederach, this means that conflict requires reconciliation, not simply the focus on interests of the parties or the cessation of peace.

Like Gülen, Lederach focuses on dialogue as key to reconciliation and transformation. However, he roots transformation in perception and subsequent practice in the capacity to "talk to ourselves" — to have an internal dialogue. Space for this is rarely created within organizations, as part of the normal professional reflection, and Lederach argues that without such "personal space," dialogue with others is less successful. Lederach draws on psychotherapeutic research suggesting that public conflicts are the external representation of internal conflicts (personal and cultural). The process of reconciliation has to address this. Dialogue, then, is complex and plural, requiring examination of the myths that provide meaning for the self or organization, and how they have been used to set polarized perception in place.

Relationships

This places relationships at the center of peacebuilding, not values or principles, with perception of the other as key. The critical questions

---

[51]   John Paul Lederach, *The Art of Peace: Interview with K. Tippett*, 2010. http://www.onbeing.org/program/art-peace/182#sthash.yNYQrYrw.dpuf.

that are asked of the other are part of what enables a different perception of the other to emerge. Imagination is key both in seeing the self and the other differently and in seeing new possibilities. Hence, for Lederach, hope is based in the dynamic of changed relationships, and the capacity to perceive things beyond and at a deeper level, through empathy. He argues that this is often seen most effectively when the web of human relationships is the focus. Imagination here begins to shade into consciousness of that web. Lederach writes of the "craft of watching webs," involving stillness, humility, and holistic awareness — not least an awareness of the physicality of the context and how this connects to feelings.[52] Key to perceiving the other as human is not simply the application of tolerance, but to see them as part of the web, requiring an awareness of the social and cultural "geography," how the web interconnects, and how we relate to the web over time. One example Lederach gives from African peacebuilding is the discovery of humanity in the other through seeing the value placed on grandchildren and the importance of legacy for them, something shared by all parties, leading to a strong sense of empathy and interdependency. It also expands the perception of time giving people a longer-term perspective. Lederach suggests the importance of developing horizontal as well as vertical spaces, such that the web of relationships is secure with leaders, but also organization members and different interest and cultural groups.

Therefore, Lederach focuses less in the development of individual character, and primarily a rational approach, and more in the relationships, perception, and achievement of reconciliation and transformation at a personal and social level. All of this chips away at narrow views of identity and community.

Serendipity

For Lederach, all-important in this transformation is the attitude of journey and discovery. This involves several things. First, the journey requires the capacity to learn as one goes along, what is referred to as

---

52 Lederach, *The Moral Imagination*, 101

serendipity. This often has a meaning of accidental learning, something that was discovered while trying to find something else, summed up by Horace Walpole who coined the term in his letter of 1754. There he makes reference to the Persian tale of the Three Princes of Serendip, who were "were always making discoveries, by accidents and sagacity, of things they were not in quest of."[53]

Sagacity takes this away from luck and into the capacity to see connections, and so to begin to understand the significance of things even whiles pursuing other ends. It is the act of a broadly attentive mind. Serendipity in peace building requires a mind focused on the goal but living in the paradox of reality. Serendipity is not caused by chance but involves the imagination of the creative mind to visualize the other and the connections. Lederach suggests that the moral imagination is central to all this, and its serendipitous appearance lies in the capacity to think peripherally, to nurture creative learning and to have flexible platforms to nurture this creativity. The first of these involved awareness of the wider environment outside the focus of any particular task. Creative learning involves seeing the creative possibilities in the connections seen. The smart flexible platforms are about developing processes and structures, which enable serendipitous learning. It might be part of any project management process, staff development, how the space is arranged in the workplace, or how the day is organized. All of this resonates with the idea of spirituality as a journey.[54]

Secondly, this involves the embracing of paradoxical curiosity and thinking. This is based again firmly in relationships rather than simply logic. Logic tends to be linear, and relationships less clear or predictable. Paradox involves capacity to hold together seemingly contradictory truths in order to locate a greater truth. The paradoxical curiosity that Lederach speaks about is the capacity to visualize the truth in the different and usually opposing viewpoints. Dealing with such paradox involves curiosity, looking to see what the meaning and implication of

---

Lederach, *The Moral Imagination*, 114

Simon Robinson, "The Spiritual Journey," *Sport and Spirituality: An Introduction*, (London: Routledge 2007): 38-57.

the paradox is. Paradoxical curiosity sustains and provokes the moral imagination. Shakespeare often uses this, not least in his comedies in which different identities are taken on, leading to broadened awareness of the self and others.[55] This is also very much like the spirit of carnival, beloved of Bakhtin,[56] in which people take on different identities, leading to incongruities and thus to learning. This is all part of the critical consciousness of different narratives in one's social environment. The holding of different aspects of the other together is close to the Jainist concept of *anekantavada*, the idea that there is no single view of the truth of a person or object. However, it is perhaps closer to Keat's idea of negative capability. In his one reference to this, he characterizes it as "when a man is capable of being in uncertainties, mysteries, doubts, without any irritable reaching after fact and reason."[57] This involves being able to see the different aspects of the other, without having to impose a single view or overall meaning. Once more for Lederach, this is founded in the awareness of the wider social web. The greater the awareness of that, the greater the possibility of finding connections that might lead to peace, not least through forgiveness. Forgiveness itself is a significant acceptance of ambiguity, that the other has both wronged one and is also able to re-establish relationships.

Paradoxical thinking is there too at the heart of the virtues that Lederach emphasizes. Alongside imagination, he argues for the importance of the gift of pessimism. Given the paradoxes noted above, one might expect this, something that is part of the critical response to meaning and practice. It is a form of systematic scepticism that is very much focused on peace building in areas of deep conflict. This is the pessimism that recognizes that deep conflict cannot be transformed easily, and therefore, easy promises are not to be trusted. This is in fact a realistic approach to sustainable change, testing the validity and sustainability of proposed creative response. Such pessimism aims not to

---

55 Some of the best examples of this are in the comedies, in which women, for different reasons, take on the identity of men, such as *Twelfth Night* and *As Your Like It*, which challenges stereotypes.
56 Mikhail, *Problems of Dostoevsky's Poetics*
57 Li Ou, *Keats and Negative Capability*, (London: Continuum, 2009): 1.

escape the past but engage it, suggesting a parallel with Aquinas' view of practical wisdom (*prudentia*[58]). The test is located in relationships sustained over time, not in formula or processes. All of this links memory, narrative, identity, and vocation. It also means attention to time and space as part of the development of a culture of peace building.[59] This further develops the idea of spiritual journey beyond the individual, because the journey, like the three princes of Serendip is made with others and in relation to others along the way, enabling dialogue. Journey also suggests intentionality — you may not know the end, but you are moving, and along the journey you are making meaning-maps of the social and physical environment.

This leads to a focus on finding voice, and Lederach's evocative idea of "voice walkers." This captures a dynamic view of integrity, developing awareness of the different voices in the social and physical environment, and finding one's own voice through dialogue and ongoing learning. At this point, Lederach comes closer to Gülen, with a focus on awareness and response. Lederach gives greater weight to the interaction with the different voices and the development of narratives. In particular, this involves "restorying"[60] as a key aspect of transformation, developing new narratives in response to the challenge and "call" of the social and physical environment.

All of this leads to on-going learning and development, with time seen not as linear but as circular, and hence as the product of continued reflection, often revisiting the same place but with different perceptions, or as Eliot puts it, knowing "the place for the first time."[61] Lederach suggests that the "soul" is found not in a dualistic aspect of the person (i.e., a non-material center of the self, found within the body), but in in these active and reflective relationships.

---

[58] Partly involving genuine openness to the past, *memoria*.

[59] Focusing on time as *Kairos*, associated with significant existential events, or moments of judgement, and the arrangement of space as mediating the significance of such events and relationships, enabling holistic dialogue.

[60] Lederach, *The Moral Imagination*, 148

[61] Thomas Stearns Eliot, "Little Gidding," *Four Quartets*, (London: Faber and Faber 1942): 14.

The development of this soul involves three things: stillness, humility, and sensuous perception. By stillness, he means pause to be open to the other. It involves the practice of attentiveness and awareness. Note this is again to do with ontology, the person, not with tools. Humility is enabled through engagement with the other, showing one's place in wider projects and narratives, involving the recognition of my relationship with the other and therefore, that the world is not summed up in my needs — the opposite of narcissism. Sensuous perception involves perception of the physicality of the space, and an appreciation of that, and often that requires a physical sense of otherness around light, color, texture, touch, or smell, such as might be found in gardens, nature, or religious buildings. This reminds us that holistic meaning is as much about the somatic (body) as about the cognitive and affective aspects of the person. The physical environment that focuses on the stimulation of difference, including color and layout, precisely develops the imagination, with allied curiosity and capacity learning, and may even have physical effects on the brain, helping the development of new brain cells.[62] The practice of these virtues leads to the finding of voice and, with that, to action.

Action

Lederach notes the importance of work that can embody meaning, much like the creative arts, which act as a bridge between feeling and thinking. The term "aesthetics" is from the Greek meaning "being sharp in the senses," i.e., being capable of grasping the connections, the web, and the beauty of relationships, to see the picture and draw the change. This locates what Lederach means by the soul of peacebuilding, something found as much in images as in analytical reflection, reinforcing the sense of meaning through physical medium and creative action. This focus on the aesthetic and moral imagination further enables an awareness of vocation. This ties in directly with responsibility because it is recognizing the human calling of the other, setting up accountabil-

---

[62] John Eberhard, *Brain Landscape*, (Oxford: Oxford University Press, 2009).

ity to the other and responsibility for the other, without prescribing what that means.

Peacebuilding then looks to establish a quality of transcendence. It breaks out of difference as division. The moral imagination finds a way to transcend the seen and the common, and link to the experience of the different stakeholders involved. Pelz and Reeves note that the most powerful moments of one peace building experience in Bosnia were when the different religious groups, fragmented by the war, came together for a service of healing which focused on the sounding of bells, silenced for several years, evoking shared memories and relationships that transcended the conflict.[63] Once again, the peace building revolves around relationships, not technique. The change is often focused in unlikely places and people, with leadership even assumed by groups outside the organization or in culturally weak positions. Lederach notes several examples in Africa of women's groups that have played significant roles in peace building. For Gülen, leadership tends to stay fixed in the Movement, with very clear and effective ways of developing service in action, but little negotiation of power and responsibilities with other groups. Lederach focuses on social transformation as a whole, not simply the development of the community or a part of the community. Hence, it looks to multiple dialogues and processes at different levels and in different social spaces taking place at the same time. As a post-conflict peacebuilder, Lederach is looking for a critical mass that involves ownership by different groups.

Lederach focuses on what he terms "imaginative meditative capacity," the awareness of the social environment and the possibilities that emerge from the relationships and the interconnections. The focus in terms of spirituality is about enabling meaning to emerge from the different narratives and the different connections, holding together difference and sameness. This takes away from the idea of peacebuilding, as focused in a single trained professional, and moves the individual and groups accepting their responsibility for peace. Hence, Lederach main-

---

[63] Peter Pelz, and Donald Reeves, *The White House: From Fear to a Handshake*, (London: O Publications, 2008).

tains, "the perspective of meditative capacity focuses attention on introducing a quality of interaction into a strategic set of social spaces within the web of systemic relationships in order to promote construc-tive change processes in the conflict-affected setting as a whole."[64] Led-erach suggests that this is less about critical mass in terms of volume and more about critical "yeast," focusing on the quality of the peace-building relationships.[65]

Peacebuilding, then, has real parallels with creative art. The peace-builder, and by extension the peacebuilders, are looking to create out-comes that will affect the whole of society. This means ensuring that the different groups at different levels of civil society and government connect and take on leadership roles, and work together at shaping and being shaped, leading to a work that is owned by them and yet not, as it has a life of its own.[66] The action is actual and symbolic, and like music or art, has the power to move, give significant meaning, remind us of shared humanity, and challenge us. Hence, such creativity has a tremendous transformative power. This cannot be forced, but is worked through in its own time. The work of peacebuilding and social change thus moves beyond analytical techniques and taps into people's more artistic, creative selves.

Conclusion

Gülen and Lederach are kindred spirits, not least because they focus on humanity and how humanity can begin to respond to and shape the social and physical environment in all its ambiguity. Gülen gives the impression of being careful (safe, thorough, and focused in care) in his peacebuilding, which enables the development of virtues such as toler-ance, compassion, and wisdom, and focuses on commitment and ser-vice in action, not least through the development of schools. He targets the evils of ignorance, poverty, and disunity and shows us clear path-

---

[64] Lederach, *The Moral Imagination*, 97

[65] Lederach, *The Moral Imagination*, 91)

[66] W.K. Wimsatt Jr., *The Verbal Icon: Studies in the Meaning of Poetry*, (Kentucky: University of Kentucky Press, 1954).

ways. Through this, he offers hope based on a positive view of humanity. Placing schools in areas of conflict is not without risk, but the process has been worked through. Moreover, it is a process that seeks to set the grounds for peace and the skills of peacebuilding in place so that it will influence the future. This does not directly try to transform the future or try to engage others in that transformation. Such transformation might well happen to the parents of Macodenian children, for instance, but that is not the specific intention. Hence, for Gülen and the *Hizmet* Movement, the aim is to keep faith with the core pathways.

In contrast, Lederach provides an almost mystical picture in which risk is central. The journey does not have a specific plan but enables, through dialogue and learning on the way, the voices to gain strength, and an openness to the possibilities of working with the largest possible number of groups. Here the intention is the transformation of society — not spelled out in terms of an ideology, but owned by all. In this, while Gülen focuses on virtues, and is thus equally focused on the person rather than the technique, Lederach spends more time on flagging up the nature of holistic spirituality. For him, rationality demands critical testing of people and projects as much as positive perception, and a rich consciousness of the place of physicality and action in relational meaning, hence the focus on peacebuilder as creative artist. Lederach describes the "moral imagination" as the capacity to recognize turning points and possibilities in order to venture down unknown paths and create what does not yet exist. There is a real risk and uncertainty in this that has to be managed, paralleled in the risk of letting go of power to others in the peace process, often to those with much less power.

Nonetheless, despite the lack of clear pathways in comparison to Gülen, there is also an intentionality in Lederach's approach to peacebuilding that is focused in finding ways to challenge and transcend destructive perceptions and patterns. Unlike Gülen then, this leads Lederach to engage more directly with the different groups in society, enabling a bigger picture of co-creation. Hence, while Gülen and the *Hizmet* Movement explore and practice creative dialogue, Lederach extends that dialogue, enabling perhaps even more mutuality, in an overarching approach to peacebuilding.

Both, however, dare to locate peace and peacebuilding at the center of the human enterprise, as something for which all are responsible. In so doing, they locate the search for peace at the heart of every debate and action.[67]

References

Bakhtin, Mikhail. *Problems of Dostoevsky's Poetics* Minneapolis, MN: University of Minnesota, 1929.

Berlin, Isaiah. "Two Concept of Liberty." A, Quinton ed. *Political Philosophy.* Oxford: Oxford University Press (1969): 141-153.

Boutros-Ghali, Boutros. *An Agenda for Peace Preventive diplomacy, peacemaking and peace-keeping*, 1992. http://www.un.org/en/peacebuilding/pbso/pbun.shtml

Bohm, David. *On Dialogue.* London: Routledge, 1996.

Bruininks, Patricia, and Bertram Malle. "Distinguishing Hope from Optimism and Related Affective States," *Motivation and Emotion*, 29, no. 4 (2005): 327-355.

De Bolt, Darian. "Dialogue: Greek foundations and the thought of Fethullah Gülen and Jürgen Habermas." Conference proceedings of Islam in the Contemporary World. *The Fethullah Gülen Movement in Thought and Practice*. Rice University: Houston, 2005.

Ebaugh, Helen Rose. *The Gülen Movement: A Sociological Analysis of a Civic Movement Rooted in Moderate Islam.* London: Springer, 2009.

Eberhard, John. *Brain Landscape.* Oxford: Oxford University Press, 2009.

Eliot, Thomas Stearns. "Little Gidding." *Four Quartets.* London: Faber and Faber (1942): 14.

Esposito, John, and Ihsan Yilmaz eds. *Islam and Peacebuilding: Gülen Movement Initiatives.* New York: Blue Dome, 2010.

Friere, Paulo. *Pedagogy of the Oppressed.* New York: Continuum, 1972.

Gizelis, Theodora. "Gender Empowerment and United Nations Peacebuilding." *Journal of Peace Research*, 46, no. 4 (2009): 505-523.

---

[67] See Judge Mervyn King (King III) and his focus on the use of ADR approaches in governance.

Graskemper, Michael. "A Bridge to Interreligious Cooperation: The Gulen-Jesuits Educational Nexus." Yilmaz, I. et al (eds.) *Muslim World in Transition: Contributions of the Gulen Movement.* London: Leeds Metropolitan University Press (2007): 622-631.

Grinell, Klas. "Border Thinking: Fethullah Gulen and the East West Divide." J. Esposito and I. Yilmaz eds. *Islam and Peacebuilding: Gülen Movement Initiatives.* New York: Blue Dome (2010): 65-84.

Gülen, Fethullah. "Sorumluluk Suuru." *Yeni Ümit Magazine,* (July-September 1995): 29.

Gülen, Fethullah. *Key Concepts in the Practice of Sufism,* 1. Fairfax: The Fountain, 1999.

Gülen, Fethullah. *Towards a Global Civilization of Love and Tolerance.* New Jersey: The Light, 2004.

Gülen, Fethullah. *Essays, Perspectives, Opinions.* Second revised edition. Somerset, N.J.: The Light, 2006.

Gürbüz, Mustafa. "Performing Moral Opposition: Musings on the Strategy and Identity in the Gülen Movement." Ihsan Yilmaz et al (eds). *Muslim World in Transition: Contributions of the Gülen Movement.* London: Leeds Metropolitan University Press (2007): 104-117.

King III. *IOD Report on Corporate Governance.* Johannesburg: IOD South Africa, 2009.

Habermas, Jürgen. *The Theory of Communicative Action.* Boston: Beacon Press, 1984.

Hefner, Robert ed. "Introduction: Modernity and the Remaking of Muslim Politics." *Remaking Muslim Politics: Pluralism, Contestation, Democratization.* Princeton: Princeton University Press, 2005.

Huntington, Samuel. *The Clash of Civilizations and the Remaking of World Order.* New York: Touchstone, 1998.

Kalyoncu, Mehmet. "Building Civil Society in Ethno-Religiously Fractured Communities: The Case of the Gülen Movement in Turkey and Abroad." Ihsan Yilmaz et al (eds). *Muslim World in Transition: Contributions of the Gülen Movement.* London: Leeds Metropolitan University Press (2007): 597-607.

Kalyoncu, Mehmet. "Gülen-inspired Schools in the East Africa: Secular Alternative in Kenya and Pragmatist Approach to Development in Uganda." *Islam in the Age of Global Challenges: Alternative Perspectives of the Gülen Movement Conference Proceedings.* Georgetown University, Washington, November 14th and November 15th 2008, Washington DC: Rumi Forum (2008): 350-373.

Kucukcan, Talip. "Social and Spiritual Capital of the Gülen Movement." Ihsan Yilmaz et al (eds.) *Muslim World in Transition: Contributions of the Gülen Movement.* London: Leeds Metropolitan University Press (2007): 187-197.

Lederach, John Paul. *The Moral Imagination.* Oxford: Oxford University Press, 2005.

Lederach, John Paul. *The Art of Peace: Interview with K. Tippett,* 2010. http://www.onbeing.org/program/art-peace/182#sthash.yNYQrYrw.dpuf.

Lester, Andrew. *Hope in Pastoral Care and Counselling.* Louisville: John Knox Press, 1995.

Michel, Thomas. "Fighting Poverty with Kimse Yok Mu?" *Islam in the Age of Global Challenges: Alternative Perspectives of the Gülen Movement Conference Proceedings.* Georgetown University, Washington, November 14th and November 15th 2008, Washington DC: Rumi Forum (2008): 350-373.

Mitchell, George. *Making Peace: The Inside Story of the Making of the Good Friday Agreement.* London: Heinemann, *1999.*

Mohamed, Yasien. "The Ethical Theory of Fethullah Gulen and its Practice in South Africa." Yilmaz et al (eds.) *The Muslim World In Transition.* London: Leeds Metropolitan University Press, 2007.

Musser, Donald, and Dixon Sunderland. *War or Words: Interreligious Dialogue as an Instrument of Peace.* Cleveland: The Pilgrim Press (2005): 1.

Novak, Michael. *Morality, Capitalism and Democracy* London: IEA, 1990.

Nursi, Bediuzzaman Said-i. "Divan-i Harb-i orfi." *Rasle-I Nur.* Istanbul: Nesil, 1996.

Ou, Li. *Keats and Negative Capability.* London: Continuum, (2009): 9.

Park, William. "The Fethullah Gulen Movement." *The Middle Eastern Review of International Affairs* 12, no 3 (2008): 1-11.

Pelz, Peter, and Donald Reeves. *The White House: From Fear to a Handshake.* London: O Publications, 2008.

Pratt, Douglas. "Islamic Prospects for Interreligious Dialgue: The Voice of Fethullah Gülen." J. Esposito and I. Yilmaz eds. *Islam and Peacebuilding: Gülen Movement Initiatives.* New York: Blue Dome, (2010): 189-206.

Ricoeour, Paul. *Onself as Another.* Chicago: Chicago University Press, 1992.

Robinson, Simon. "The Spiritual Journey." J. Parry et al, eds. *Sport and Spirituality: An Introduction.* London: Routledge (2007): 38-57.

Robinson, Simon. *Spirituality, Ethics and Care.* Joanna Kingsley: London, 2008.

Saritoprak, Zeki. "Gülen and his Global Contribution to Peacebuilding." Ihsan Yilmaz et al (eds.) *Muslim World in Transition: Contributions of the Gülen Movement.* London: Leeds Metropolitan University Press (2007): 632-642.

Robinson, Simon. "Islam Responsibility and Business." M. Farrar, S. Robinson, Y. Valli, and P. Wetherly eds. *Islam In the West.* Basingstoke: Plagrave (2012): 154-168.

Sarıtoprak, Zeki. "Fethullah Gülen's Theology of Peacebuilding." J. Esposito and I. Yilmaz eds. *Islam and Peacebuilding: Gülen Movement Initiatives.* New York: Blue Dome (2010): 169-188.

Synder, C.R. "The past and possible futures of hope." *Journal of Social and Clinical Psychology* 19, no. 1 (Spring 2000): 11-28.

Ünal, Ali, and Alphonse Williams. *Advocate of Dialogue: Fethullah Gulen.* Fairfax, Virginia: Fountain, 2009.

CHAPTER THREE

TOLERANCE IN THE THEOLOGY AND THOUGHT OF A. J. CONYERS AND FETHULLAH GÜLEN

David B. Capes

Introduction

In his book *The Long Truce: How Toleration Made the World Safe for Profit and Power*[1] the late A. J. Conyers argues that tolerance, as it has developed in Western, post-Reformation democracies, is not a public virtue but rather a political strategy employed to centralize power and guarantee profits. Tolerance, of course, seemed to be a reasonable response to the religious wars of the 16th and 17th centuries, but tolerance based on indifference to all values except political power and materialism has relegated ultimate questions of meaning to private life. Conyers offers another model for tolerance based on values and resources already resident in pre-Reformation Christianity.

In this essay, I consider aspects of Conyers' case against the modern, secular doctrine of tolerance. I examine his attempt to reclaim the practice of Christian tolerance based on humility, hospitality, and the "powerful fact" of the incarnation. Furthermore, I bring the late Conyers into dialogue with Fethullah Gülen, a Muslim scholar, prolific writer, and source of inspiration for a transnational civil movement. I

---

[1] A.J. Conyers, *The Long Truce: How Toleration Made the World Safe for Profit and Power,* (Dallas: Spence Publishing, 2001).

explore how both Conyers and Gülen interpret their scriptures and tradition in order to fashion a theology and political ideology conducive to peaceful co-existence.[2]

Until his untimely death at the age of 60, Conyers had distinguished himself as a gifted Baptist theologian with an ever-increasing audience.[3] He was a consummate, "southern gentleman" (in the American sense of the word), kind, welcoming, and sincere. As a scholar, he benefited from a positive relationship with Jürgen Moltmann, whose influence appears consistently, though not uncritically, in his work.[4] As a Baptist, Conyers was a member of a denomination in the U.S. that is not typically associated with tolerance but has strong convictions, passion, and fervency in faith. Still, despite popular perceptions, there is a significant tradition of tolerance and freedom of conscience among many Baptist thinkers in Europe, beginning with Thomas Helwys. Baptists, of course, were a religious minority at the turn of the 17th century, so they faced hostility from both established churches and government officials. As a result, they advocated for religious liberty initially for themselves but by extension for all. They formulated the doctrine directly from Christian Scripture, reason, and human experience. Essentially,

---

[2] My assumption for this presentation is that A. J. Conyers and his work are relatively unknown to the audience. On the other hand, the contributions of Gülen are well known to most if not all readers. However, for a helpful overview of Gülen's life, see Ali Ünal and Alphonse Williams, *Advocate of Dialogue: Fethullah Gülen* (Fairfax, VA: Fountain, 2000), 1-42.

[3] A.J. (Abdah Johnson) "Chip" Conyers III, Ph.D., Rev. (May 29, 1944-July, 18, 2004) was a Baptist theologian and ordained minister. He was born in San Bernardino, California. He held degrees from the University of Georgia (B.A., political science), Southeastern Baptist Theological Seminary (M.Div.), and Southern Baptist Theological Seminary (Ph.D.). His dissertation topic was "Jürgen Moltmann's Concept of History." He served for many years as a faculty member at Baylor University's George W. Truett Theological Seminary. As one of the first faculty members, Conyers was Professor of Theology at Truett Seminary where he worked until his death from cancer in 2004. Conyers was a member of First Baptist Church, Waco, Texas, and also served on the board of many ministries and was the president of the board of Christian Cultural Awareness and Assistance League (C-CAAL).

[4] A. J. Conyers, *God, Hope, and History: Jürgen Moltmann and the Christian Concept of History* (Macon, GA: Mercer University Press, 1988).

they argued that government should not meddle in matters of religion and conscience. Had they known it, they would have agreed wholeheartedly with the Qur'anic injunction that there is no compulsion in religion. Baptist leaders scandalized some by advocating religious liberty for Roman Catholics, Turks, Jews, and heretics alike,[5] as they believed religious uniformity was not necessary to ensure domestic tranquility.[6] In the last century, this Baptist distinctive is articulated carefully in the work of E. Y. Mullins,[7] and Conyers carries on that tradition, representing the most recent and articulate advocate for tolerance in American Baptist life. He also recognizes that the practice of toleration is "not an exclusively Christian predisposition, for the practice of toleration is often touchingly and effectively expressed in such religious philosophies as one finds associated with Hinduism, Taoism, Confucianism, and among the Sufi mystics of Islam."[8] This is all the more reason to bring Conyers and Gülen into conversation.

Conyers' Critique

Since the 17th century, tolerance has often been considered a public virtue. In the last decades of the 20th century tolerance/toleration became one of the principle virtues[9] institutionalized in Western democracies

---

5   Thomas Helwys, *The Mistery of Iniquity* (London: 1612), 69.

6   H. Leon McBeth, *The Baptist Heritage* (Nashville: Broadman, 1987), 85-86.

7   E.Y. Mullins, *Axioms of Religion: A New Interpretation of Baptist Faith* (American Baptist Publication Society: Philadelphia, 1908), 44, argues that Baptists historically have led out with the ideas of "soul liberty" and the "separation of church and state." In addition, Mullins sees that "[t]oleration and religious liberty are the poles apart," seeing that the "Calverts" and Roman Catholics did not go far enough in securing toleration from England, 48-49.

8   Conyers, *Truce*, 228.

9   Thomas Aquinas distinguishes the cardinal virtues, temperance, justice, prudence, and fortitude, from the theological virtues, faith, hope, and charity (*Summa Theologiae*, I-II, Q. lxi, aa. 2 and 4). The cardinal virtues are derived in the "subjects" or "faculties" of humans, whereas the theological virtues are "supernatural" and come from God. Recent philosophers like J. Budziszewski wish to see tolerance as a virtue, *True Tolerance* (New Brunswick: Transaction Publishers, 1992), 5.

in a variety of ways.[10] Conyers, however, questions whether tolerance should be considered a virtue at all. Compared with other classical virtues such as love, courage, and moderation, Conyers argues that tolerance is different because of the common acknowledgement that there must be limits on tolerance. John Locke famously argued that tolerance is not limitless;[11] some, he proposed, are not to be tolerated, including atheists and Roman Catholics. While we might disagree about where the line of toleration is drawn, everyone acknowledges that the line must be drawn somewhere. When the Boniuk Institute for the Study and Advancement of Religious Toleration at Rice University held its inaugural conference in September 2005, the theme of that conference was "Tolerance and Its Limits." In Conyers' view, true virtue has no limits. He writes:

> A virtue strengthens our relationships. From a Christian perspective, all virtues serve the interests of love, love being the chief virtue and goal of life. Humility, patience, and prudence make it possible to love God, the world, and human beings, all in their proper order and proportion. Virtues are interconnected and, in a sense, are all one. They are themselves the goal of human life. We are created for this: to be capable of loving.[12]

For Conyers, all lesser virtues serve the chief virtue of love. There is never a time when love is out of place or courage is inappropriate. But everyone agrees that tolerance cannot be limitless.

---

10 Marcuse, "Repressive Tolerance," 1, argues that tolerance is an end in itself. Marcuse, who is a Hegelian, sees history as eventually telling the "truth." So the end of this virtue itself is played out in "extralegal means," i.e., violence and revolution. The irony is in how the original purpose of tolerance, namely, to assuage the problems of religious wars in earlier centuries will climax in violence. This is one of the reasons why Conyers sees the 20th century as being the most violent. See his *The Listening Heart: Vocation and the Crisis of Modern Culture* (Spence, 2001).

11 John Locke would not extend toleration to the Roman Catholic Church and atheists, *A Letter Concerning Toleration*, trans. William Pope (1689). He gives reason that the former "deliver themselves up to the protection and the service of another prince," i.e. the Pope, and the latter are not motivated to hold to "promises, covenants, and oaths."

12 Conyers, *Truce*, 7–8.

Then what is tolerance if it is not a virtue? Conyers proffers that tolerance is a modern strategy to establish centralized power and to protect economic prosperity. While it may depend on virtues such as humility, moderation, patience, etc., tolerance is in fact a policy to achieve a particular end that is itself a good. Tolerance aims to ease the tensions rooted in the significant differences facing people in a shrinking, global world; as such, it is not an end but a means to an end, a strategy that seeks harmony and peace within our common life.[13] While Conyers advocates for peaceful co-existence as a good worthy of all our efforts, he questions whether the modern strategy of tolerance advocated in secular democracies has a sufficient basis. He bases his argument upon an analysis of key writers on tolerance including Thomas Hobbes, Pierre Bayle, John Locke, and others.[14]

Conyers begins his critique of the modern doctrine of tolerance by noting that its genesis in the thought of John Locke and John Stuart Mill arose along with the establishment of the modern nation-states.[15] Prior to that time, human societies had been composed of a variety of "natural" associations based on ethnic, religious, familial, and economic ties. These groups have their own purpose, authority structure, and internal discipline.[16] With the rise of nation-states, however, the influence of the natural associations is diminished in favor of more centralized authority. As this transpires, there is a concomitant development: a growing isolation of the individual. In the pre-modern period, identity had been constructed in relation to a group. Now, with the authority and the influence of the group eclipsed by the larger, more powerful state, identity is confused. Rather than necessary and generative to the life of a

---

13 Conyers, *Truce*, 7-8.
14 Conyers, *Truce*, 66-168.
15 Conyers defines the nation-state as "political entities taking in large territories and uniting peoples heretofore politically unrelated," *Truce*, 5.
16 Dietrich Bonhoeffer, *Ethics* (New York: Touchstone Books, 1995), 147, thinks that there is inevitable tension that exists between the natural associations and the organized state. Governments and organizations may collapse but natural associations (family, friends, religious communities) tend to continue. Natural associations may be disrupted for a time but they generally survive. For that reason natural associations are ultimately more influential.

person, these associations are construed as involuntary and accidental. According to Conyers, "the result was a powerful state and a lonely individual, two distinctive features of the modern period."[17]

While we tend to think of the world today almost exclusively in terms of large, diverse nation-states, this rather recent phenomenon brought with it significant changes to social, political and religious life. In the modern nation-state the centralization of the government depends largely on the secularization of public life. As Michael Walzer has argued, in order to establish peace, differences must be managed.[18] Generally, a single, dominant group that organizes public life in such a way as to reflect and maintain its own culture manages these differences, since unmanaged differences will inevitably "disturb the peace." Differences, especially religious differences with their ultimate claims, must be managed above all, so there are three options: (1) insist that all have the same religion; (2) forbid religion from entering the public sphere; or (3) consign religion to the private sphere. Generally, it is options 2 and 3 that have characterized Western democracies. In France and Turkey, for example, the practice of laicism has effectively excluded religion from public life. In the United States and other Western democracies, freedom of religion may be guaranteed, but ample social and legal strictures are present to consign religion effectively to the margins.

No doubt the religious wars that devastated Europe in the 16th and 17th centuries play a significant role in how modern philosophers and statesmen construct their views of tolerance,[19] but Conyers points out that the expansion of territories, the rise of powerful nation-states, and the growth of trade with its promises of wealth made Europe ripe for conflict without the stresses caused by religious differences. Clearly,

---

[17] Conyers, *Truce*, 6.

[18] Michael Walzer, *On Toleration* (New Haven: Yale University Press, 1997), 25.

[19] Immanuel Kant, *Perpetual Peace,* 1795, Constitution Society, http://www.constitution.org/kant/perpeace.htm, sees that the peace that exists between people is not "the natural state (*status naturalis*)," but he argues, "the natural state is one of war." Therefore, in order for peace to exist a pledge is required for people who exist together, which can only take place in "a civil state."

religion was not the only factor that led to the horrors of the Thirty Years War, but it was partly to blame. Modern philosophies see the dangers of religion, so they seek to remove it as a viable strategy for dealing with differences.

Conyers believes the modern doctrine of toleration has failed and will continue to fail because it bifurcates life into public and private spheres and assigns a marginal role to questions of ultimate concern.[20] While the modern doctrine of tolerance initially pretends to support the idea of religion, it almost immediately will neutralize any sincere expression of religious conviction. With one hand the tolerant democracy gives — and it can afford to give because it is a powerful, prosperous state — but with the other it takes away. The wedding of tolerance with power will ultimately mean that tolerance will give way to other kinds of intolerance.[21]

Reclaiming the Practice of Tolerance

Since the modern project of tolerance will likely fail, Conyers suggests that we must seek to reclaim the ancient practice of tolerance in order to meet the growing tensions apparent in our shrinking, global world. For those who are open to religion,[22] the practice of "high tolerance" or "authentic tolerance," as he refers to it, is natural inasmuch as it deals with ultimate questions of meaning and purpose. The modern strategy of tolerance, however, merely postpones those questions in order to privilege other, more manageable questions, but according to Conyers,

---

[20] Conyers, "Rescuing Tolerance," 43-44, recognizes that the privatization of religion was intended not only to protect the state, but religious life as well. But this resulted in the assumption that public life belonged ultimately to the state.

[21] Herbert Marcuse, "Repressive Tolerance" in *A Critique of Pure Tolerance*, ed by Robert Paul Wolff, Barrington Moore, Jr., and Herbert Marcuse (Boston: Beacon Press, 1969), 95 137.

[22] For Conyers tolerance is a theological question. Modernity has worked hard to close the door on the transcendent nature of tolerance. Ultimately, understanding tolerance is for all insofar as any discussion about tolerance is a religious discussion.

authentic tolerance must first be disentangled from the "questionable alliance with power and will to power."[23]

Conyers asks: Is there a practice of tolerance not based on indifference to the question of "the good"? Is there an authentic tolerance that does not privilege power and materialism over deeper, more abiding questions? Yes, he argues, and the answer is found in the central mystery of the incarnation.[24] For Conyers, "the powerful fact of the incarnation" provides a basis sufficient to reorder human existence and establish peace amidst difference.[25] Conyers is quick to point out, however, that he is not talking about "the doctrine of the incarnation"; for it is in the nature of doctrines to develop over time and doctrines may or may not be true. Rather, he is speaking of the central conviction that God became flesh in the particularity of Jesus of Nazareth and that He was in Christ to reconcile the world.[26]

As a "fact" or "conviction" rather than a doctrine, it is not necessary that we grasp the reality of the incarnation or can explain it in some systematic fashion. It is more important, according to Conyers, that the reality grasps us and reorients our lives essentially toward a more tolerant and open attitude toward others who share the same enfleshed existence. Incarnation then becomes the basis for hope. A life shaped by the vigorous conviction of the incarnation may well be aware that the world is filled with suffering (because of intolerance and other problems), but it also recognizes that it is not destined for suffering nor is it beyond hope. If God has entered our world and dwelt among us, then our world must be good and our future hopeful. This stands in stark contrast to the modern notion that the world is to be feared, subdued and made safe for power and profit.

If the fact of the incarnation provides hope, then the purpose of the incarnation provides reconciliation. Initially, that means reconciliation between God and humanity, but it also means reconciliation between people for whom differences have proven to be difficult and often

---

23 Conyers, *Truce*, 229.
24 Conyers, *Truce*, 231.
25 Conyers, *Truce*, 232.
26 Conyers, *Truce*, 232.

insurmountable problems. Reconciliation in practice manifests itself in tolerance and openness to "the other."[27] Conyers argues that the Church is "the natural culture" for reclaiming an authentic practice of toleration despite the impulses that have led some to legitimate violence through religion. If God was in Christ reconciling the world (2 Cor. 5:16), then the reconciliation of all things (*ta panta*) becomes the *raison d'etre* of the Church. Ultimately, the incarnation means that all things are interrelated. Therefore, all things must matter to God, and all things must include all people. In Christ, God loved the world — we are part of that world and so is "the other."[28]

The incarnation also reveals something hitherto unknown regarding God and humanity. In Christ's self-emptying and death on the cross (Phil. 2:5-11), his followers see a "lordly example" of humility and are called to imitate it.[29] Therefore, according to Conyers, the practice of the incarnation is first of all the practice of humility that manifests itself in listening to others. This does not mean listening for the sake of gaining advantage or seeking information; this is listening expectantly, waiting to hear the truth.[30] Conyers surveys the biblical evidence for toleration and defines it as: "a willingness to hear other traditions and learn from them"[31] Indeed, the fundamental virtue necessary for tolerance to exist and flourish is humility. This kind of authentic tolerance reflects a depth to humility that is willing to set aside the self to attend to the voice of "the other." Humility then, for Conyers, is what makes dialogue possible.

Dialogue birthed in authentic tolerance is not content to dwell on similarities, agreements, and surface issues; it begins with commonalities but does not stop until it has engaged the most cherished and deeply held convictions of a group, even when those convictions differ con-

---

27 Conyers, *Truce*, 241.
28 Conyers, *Truce*, 234.
29 L. W. Hurtado, "Jesus as Lordly Example in Philippians 2:5-11," in *From Jesus to Paul: Studies in Honour of Francis Wright Beare*, ed Peter Richardson and John C. Hurd (Waterloo, Ontario: Wilfrid Laurier University Press, 1984), 113-126.
30 Conyers, *Truce*, 233.
31 Conyers, *Truce*, 33.

siderably from people to people. This kind of dialogue stands in sharp relief to the pseudo-toleration that makes "dialogue possible only so long as it conforms to certain `rules' that preordain its result."[32] Conyers remarks:

> Just as pseudo-toleration answers power with power, it answers bigotry with bigotry. The hallmark of authentic tolerant practice should be the listening heart for which the wise king prayed and not the management of language and appointing itself the arbiter of all public discussions.[33]

Elsewhere Conyers refers to this tolerant disposition toward "the other" as *the practice of the open soul*. He writes:

> Such toleration reaches outward toward an ecumenical goal, with eternity as its ultimate horizon, because its practice is essentially the practice of the open soul. It springs not from the fear and self-protection that Thomas Hobbes was so sure animated all things in human society where life is naturally "solitary, poor, nasty, brutish and short," but it springs from a propensity toward magnanimity and a predisposition toward faith. The recovery of this *practice of toleration* would mark the reversal of a very old prejudice in the modern mind. It would reverse the deep-seated suspicion that undergirds much of modern thought, the suspicion that the world cannot be known, much less loved, and that it must be conquered in order to be made safe.[34]

The practice of the open soul is essentially the practice of hospitality. It involves "welcoming the stranger" and serving his/her physical, social, and spiritual needs. In any cross-cultural exchange both parties are strangers, aliens to the other, so hospitality involves not only giving but also receiving in a way that gives dignity and honor to the other. As

---

[32] Conyers, *Truce*, 244.
[33] Conyers, *Truce*, 244. Often translations of 1 Kings 3:9 indicate that Solomon prays for "wisdom," but the Hebrew phrase means literally "listening heart."
[34] Conyers, *Truce*, 245.

Amy Oden has written: "Acts of inclusion and respect, however small, can powerfully reframe social relations and engender welcome."[35]

It is important to note that Conyers considers "high tolerance," as he refers to it, a recovery or reclaiming of what the Church practiced in earlier days. He finds significant evidence that Christian believers in earlier centuries exercised tolerance and openness, though not universally. He notes in particular the writings of Justin Martyr (d. 165), Clement of Alexandria (d. 215), and Thomas Aquinas (ca. 1225-1274). Justin, he notes, associated the *Logos* of Greek philosophy with the Christ and made possible a link from the earliest, pre-Christian philosophers to Christian theology. Similarly, Clement incorporated the best of Greek literature and philosophy into his own writings.[36] According to Conyers, Thomas Aquinas' *Summa Theologiae* — one of the greatest achievements in Christian thought and history — "would never have seen the light of day but for a strong sentiment for a certain openness toward thinkers from other faiths and other philosophies."[37] In particular on the question of "truth" (*Summa Theologiae*, XVI "On Truth"), Aquinas draws from Christian, Jewish, Muslim, and "pagan" teachers, but he does not draw on these thinkers in any sort of modern way. Conyers remarks:

> What are we to make of this unpretentious move by Saint Thomas, in a work of Christian theology, from the church fathers, to medieval Christians, to a Muslim, to a pagan? There is no self-conscious celebration of diversity here, not even the thought of it. Nor is there the resigned air of "everyone is entitled to one's own opinion, since no one can gainsay opinion." Just the opposite is the case, in fact, because there is the resolute pressing forward to an idea of truth that is common to everyone simply because it is *real* for everyone. It is inclusive

---

[35] Amy G. Oden, ed. *And You Welcomed Me: A Sourcebook on Hospitality in Early Christianity* (Nashville: Abingdon, 2001), 14. See also Christine D. Pohl, *Making Room: Recovering Hospitality as a Christian Tradition* (Grand Rapids: Eerdmans, 1999).

[36] Conyers, *Truce*, 34-36.

[37] A. J. Conyers, "Rescuing Tolerance," *First Things: A Monthly Journal of Religion & Public Life*, 115 (Aug/ Sep 2001): 43-46.

not in the easy modern way that makes its claim before any effort has been expended to find common ground but in the more arduous medieval way.[38]

Conyers, of course, is not alone in this assessment. David Burrell suggests that the doctrine of God inherited by the enlightened West was already an achievement of interfaith dialogue.[39]

Conyers and Gülen

Although A. J. Conyers and Fethullah Gülen were shaped in different worlds culturally and religiously — and I find no evidence that one influenced the other — amazing resonance exists between them on this issue of tolerance. This resonance is located precisely in the vitality of their respective faiths. For both men, their deep religious commitment informs their unwavering commitment to tolerance.[40] Still, there are subtle differences between them based in large part upon the faith communities and worlds from which they come.

First, it must be acknowledged that both Gülen and Conyers are working from a similar definition of toleration. Gülen defines tolerance as embracing all people regardless of differences and having the ability to put up with matters we personally dislike by drawing upon the strength of convictions, conscience, faith and a generous heart.[41] One of the key concepts Gülen uses in discussions of tolerance is *hoshgoru* (*hosh* = good, pleasant; *goru* = view). Sometimes this word is translated into English as "tolerance," but conceptually it is probably best taken as empathetic acceptance. For Gülen, tolerance involves identifying with and accepting others, but one cannot identify with others without first listening to them and understanding the world from which they come. Conyers would agree with this construal of tolerance and go on to say

---

[38] Conyers, *Truce*, 233.

[39] David Burrell, *Knowing the Unknowable God: Ibn-Sina, Maimonides, Aquinas* (Notre Dame: University of Notre Dame Press, 1986), ix.

[40] On the paradox of commitment and tolerance in Gülen, see Lester R. Kurtz, "Gülen's Paradox: Combining Commitment and Tolerance," *The Muslim World* 95.3 (July 2005), 373-384.

[41] Gülen, *Love & Tolerance*, p. 46.

that difference is what makes "high tolerance" possible. Unlike some moderns who may wish to eliminate differences and seek to assimilate minority groups into the powerful state, Gülen and Conyers argue that embracing differences ultimately serves the same goal and demonstrates respect for those who otherwise would be left out.[42] Furthermore, both Gülen and Conyers locate the resources necessary to create an atmosphere of tolerance precisely in the particularity of each faith community. For Gülen, the essence of Islam — like the word "Islam" — involves surrender [to God], peace, contentment and security. He cites a well-known episode from the life of the Prophet: When asked what practice of the faith is most beneficial, Muhammad remarks that feeding the hungry and offering *salaam* (the greeting of peace) to both friend and stranger are the most beneficial.[43] Essentially, the pursuit of peace and seeking to establish peace are fundamental to Islam. If "peace is better" as the Qur'an teaches (4:128), then the true Muslim will work toward peace. Likewise, Conyers argues from a Christian perspective that the pursuit of peace via authentic tolerance is implicitly theological.[44] If the modern project of tolerance sets aside faith and ultimate questions about humanity, the world, and God because these questions cannot be easily resolved, then authentic tolerance deals precisely with these questions and embraces those who answer the questions differently.[45] The pursuit of peace is therefore an essential call for any Christ-follower as it is for any Muslim.

For Gülen, tolerance is ultimately rooted in the attributes of God. God is All-Forgiving, All-Merciful, and All-Compassionate. These attributes of God, while common to the teaching of all the messengers of the past, have been communicated most effectively through the Qur'an and

---

[42] Other words for tolerance include respect, mercy, generosity, and forbearance. Tolerance is the "most essential element of moral systems." Gülen, *Love & Tolerance*, 33.

[43] Gülen, *Love & Tolerance*, 58.

[44] Gülen, *Love & Tolerance*, 25.

[45] Within the Christian tradition, for example, Jesus is known as "the Prince of Peace" based primarily upon the strength of an intertextual appropriation of Isa 9:6 to him. Likewise, Jesus teaches his disciples: "Blessed are the peacemakers for they will be called the sons of God" (Matt 5:9).

the Sunna. In particular, the Qur'an calls all Muslims to engage in tolerance and forgiveness because of the nature of God (64:14). Although a true believer may defend himself from attack, God does not forbid showing kindness and acting justly to those non-Muslims who are willing to live in peace (60:8). True believers are called to forgive those who do not look forward to the Days of God (45:14). Likewise, they are to swallow their anger and forgive others when they have been harmed (3:134). Gülen cites these passages, along with many others, to show that the Qur'an itself is "the source of leniency and tolerance."[46] Additionally, Gülen relates a number of episodes from the life of the Prophet and his companions to show that he was a man of peace and demonstrated peace in his relationships with friends, enemies, and People of the Book.[47] The negative statements about Jews and Christians in the Qur'an, according to Gülen, are not universal injunctions. They are sourced in contingent circumstances of doctrinal controversies or active hostilities. Clearly, the Qur'an criticizes certain beliefs held by Jews and Christians (e.g., claiming God has a son and granting certain powers to the clergy). However, these critiques are leveled against ideas and attitudes, not people. Furthermore, those verses that permit fighting are based on the active hostilities of particular Jewish, Christian, or pagan groups against the nascent Muslim community. On the whole, according to Gülen, the Qur'an is balanced toward civilized, peaceful coexistence while preserving Muslim identity.[48]

One of the strongest points of connection between Gülen and Conyers on tolerance resides in their conviction that faith in the One God reveals the interrelatedness of all things. Gülen begins with the idea that love is the reason for creation and existence, and that everything in the world is God's handiwork. Accordingly, if one does not approach

---

[46] *Love & Tolerance*, 37-38. See the collection of Qur'anic passages cited by Gülen in Alp Aslandogan, "Interfaith Dialog and Tolerance in the Contemporary World: Fethullah Gülen," (paper presented to the Southwest Commission on Religious Studies in Dallas, TX in March 2007).

[47] Ibid., 41-44.

[48] I am grateful to Dr. Alp Alsandogan for helping me understand this point of Gülen's teaching.

all humans, who are creatures of God, with love, then one hurts those who love God and those whom God loves. Essentially, one cannot claim to love God without loving everything that God has made. Love, of course, is an essential pillar of tolerance.[49] Similarly, Conyers would agree with Gülen's teaching on love and the interrelatedness of all things, but once again, for him, the incarnation informs the discussion because it reveals God's love for all things and ultimately reconciles all things back to God. If all things are destined to be reconciled to God, then the believers' vocation in this age consists of joining God in "the ministry of reconciliation" (2 Cor. 5:16-20).

The interrelatedness of all things leads Gülen to practice what Conyers calls in his theology the "open soul." Gülen has famously said: "Be so tolerant that our heart becomes wide like the ocean. Become inspired with faith and love for others. Offer a hand to those in trouble, and be concerned about everyone."[50] For Gülen, faith in God and love for God's creation serve as twin pillars for a tolerance that makes one's heart as wide as the ocean. Practically, this is worked out in deeds of generosity, compassion, and hospitality directed to everyone, regardless of their need. Similarly, Gülen has said: "Applaud the good for their goodness, appreciate those who have believing hearts, and be kind to believers. Approach unbelievers so gently that their envy and hatred melt away."[51] Gülen does not limit the word "believers" to Muslims, but to People of the Book (Jews and Christians) and by extension all people. He bases this upon the Qur'anic injunction that calls Muslims to accept the earlier prophets and their books (2:2-4) and to act kindly and justly toward non-Muslims as long as they are not fighting against them (60:8). However, such openness must also be balanced when it comes to oppressors. Gülen warns that there are limits to tolerance and dialogue when he writes: "Being merciful to a cobra means being unjust to the people the cobra has bitten."[52]

---

[49] Kurtz, 375-382.
[50] F. Gülen, *Pearls of Wisdom* (New Jersey: Light), 75.
[51] Gülen, *Pearls*, 75.
[52] Gülen, *Love & Tolerance*, 75-76.

The practice of "the open soul" for both Gülen and Conyers depends upon humility. Humility for Gülen means judging "your worth in the Creator's sight by how much space He occupies in your heart and your worth in people's eyes by how you treat them."[53] We see in this statement evidence of the spiritual side of Islam, a kind of mysticism typical of the Sufi tradition.

The human heart is made for its Creator and is at its best (namely, humble and generous) when the All-forgiving and All-merciful One fills every corner. Gülen privileges the spiritual sphere of Islam over the institutional and political spheres. This means that one's commitment to vitality in his/her spiritual life manifests itself in treating others with compassion, forgiveness, love, and tolerance.[54] Such treatment will be noticed and appreciated, and it will result in kind treatment in return.

As we saw earlier in this essay, Conyers also considers humility fundamental to any authentic practice of tolerance, but as a Christian, Conyers locates that virtue in the example of Christ and the call to "follow" him. Additionally, Conyers finds that the reality of the incarnation challenges every idea and practice of *exousia* ("power" or "authority"). In the New Testament, Jesus is clearly a prophet with authority and he shares that authority with his disciples, yet the teaching here is "not simply one of power distributed from on high but power exercised as a cosmic exchange. It is not the love of power but the power of love: God has become man, and that man, the representative of the race of men, is indeed God, so that human beings can participate in all that God is."[55] For Conyers, the coming of Christ into the world is a powerful demonstration of God's love for us, a love that ultimately exalts those who are truly humble. As the Scripture says: "God opposes the proud, but gives grace to the humble" (Jas. 4:6, quoting Prov. 3:34).

For both Gülen and Conyers, the practice of tolerance with roots firmly planted in their respective Scriptures and traditions finds its *telos* in dialogue, what Conyers calls "the listening heart," but Gülen has

---

[53]   Ibid., 31.

[54]   Kurtz, 376-378.

[55]   Conyers, *Truce*, 238.

been able to accomplish more than any leader or activist I know to inspire a generation of leaders who have taken the message of love, tolerance, and dialogue to the nations. In particular, Gülen has urged his followers to found organizations committed to dialogue and tolerance. He has recommended that tolerance awards be given to encourage leaders from a variety of faith communities to work toward peaceful co-existence. He has warned that tolerance and dialogue will be costly ventures and that changing the social landscape will take decades.[56] For Gülen, interfaith dialogue involves people who are committed to their faith coming together and bearing witness to that faith for the express purpose of mutual understanding, empathy, appreciation, enrichment, and cooperation.[57] Dialogue is not about proselytizing or attempting to convert others. It is not about debating the merits or various truth claims of each faith. It is not an attempt to unify all faiths or create a single, world religion. It is also not about compromising one's own faith.[58] Those who approach dialogue with hidden agendas will find the engagement frustrating, polarizing, and ultimately a failure. Successes in interfaith dialogue will come slowly, as sincere individuals share the stories that have shaped their lives. By learning the truth about others and their faiths, by respecting the differences that exist between all of God's creation, we find our own faiths enriched, our commitments deepened, and perhaps we will create a world where peace reigns.

Conclusion

While Gülen and Conyers share much in common in relation to their theology of tolerance, I find one significant difference between them.

---

[56] Gülen, *Love & Tolerance*, 41, 54-57. No doubt Conyers' illness and premature death prevented him from realizing many of the goals he set out for himself. His work with the Christian Cultural Awareness League (C-CAL) was just beginning when he was diagnosed with cancer. The last decade of his life was spent fighting a disease that would ultimately take his life.

[57] Alsandogan, "Interfaith Dialog and Tolerance in the Contemporary World: Fethullah Gülen."

[58] Gülen, *Love & Tolerance*, 42.

Gülen understands the crucial roles that forgiveness and non-retaliation play in creating sacred spaces where tolerance can flourish. He refers to forgiveness as a great virtue that is paramount to tolerance. Forgiveness restores us and our world in ways that no other action can. To be forgiven is to be repaired, yet one cannot seek forgiveness without forgiving others, for "the road to forgiveness passes through the act of forgiving."[59] However, like tolerance, there are limits to forgiveness. To forgive "monstrous, evil" people who delight in suffering would be disrespectful to forgiveness itself. Furthermore, we have no right to forgive such people; to forgive them is to disrespect the people who have suffered so much from them. Similarly, a person committed to tolerance must also be committed to non-retaliation. According to Gülen, tolerance will manifest itself in halting verbal attacks or abuse of unbelievers. True Muslims will swallow their anger and forgive as the Qur'an teaches (3:134). Citing the Sufi leader, Yunus, Gülen encourages those who have been attacked to act as if they had no hand or tongue with which to strike back.[60] Clearly, for Gülen, forgiveness and a commitment to non-retaliation are foundational to tolerance.

I am unable to find an explicit discussion of forgiveness and non-retaliation relating to tolerance in Conyers' writings. While I think these two commitments may be implicit in his emphasis on humility, openness, and the reconciliation that comes through Christ, the fact is that Conyers does not mention them unambiguously in his attempt to reclaim the ancient practice. This, in my view, is a significant oversight that may be credited to the insulated academic and ecclesiastical environments in which many European and American theologians have worked. Gülen, on the other hand, has labored in a world where injustice and suffering are the ambient reality, where retaliation is natural, and where forgiveness is only a distant hope.

If Conyers had ever spent time with Gülen, I am confident he would have come away from those conversations enriched and with a friend and co-worker in the cause of peace. Both men are effective advocates of dialogue and tolerance precisely because of their commitment to their faiths.

---

[59] Gülen, *Love & Tolerance*, 27-30.
[60] Gülen, *Love & Tolerance*, 61.

Works Cited

Aslandogan, Alp. "Interfaith Dialog and Tolerance in the Contemporary World: Fethullah Gülen." Paper presented to the Southwest Commission on Religious Studies in Dallas, TX in March 2007.

Bonhoeffer, Dietrich. *Ethics*. New York: Touchstone Books, 1995.

Burrell, David. *Knowing the Unknowable God: Ibn-Sina, Maimonides, Aquinas*. Notre Dame: University of Notre Dame Press, 1986.

Conyers, A. J. *God, Hope, and History: Jürgen Moltmann and the Christian Concept of History*. Macon, GA: Mercer University Press, 1988.

Conyers, A. J. "Rescuing Tolerance." *First Things: A Monthly Journal of Religion & Public Life* 115 (Aug/ Sep 2001): 43-46.

Conyers, A.J. *The Long Truce: How Toleration Made the World Safe for Profit and Power*. Dallas: Spence Publishing, 2001.

Gülen, Fethullah. *Pearls of Wisdom*. New Jersey: Light.

Helwys, Thomas. *The Mistery of Iniquity*. London: 1612.

Hurtado, L. W. "Jesus as Lordly Example in Philippians 2:5-11." *From Jesus to Paul: Studies in Honour of Francis Wright Beare*, ed. Peter Richardson and John C. Hurd. Waterloo, Ontario: Wilfrid Laurier University Press. (1984): 113-126.

Kant, Immanuel. *Perpetual Peace*. 1795, Constitution Society, http://www.constitution.org/kant/perpeace.htm

Marcuse, Herbert. "Repressive Tolerance." *A Critique of Pure Tolerance*, ed by Robert Paul Wolff, Barrington Moore, Jr., and Herbert Marcuse. Boston: Beacon Press. (1969): 95-137.

McBeth, H. Leon. *The Baptist Heritage*. Nashville: Broadman, 1987.

Mullins, E.Y. *Axioms of Religion: A New Interpretation of Baptist Faith*. American Baptist Publication Society: Philadelphia, 1908.

Oden, Amy G. ed. *And You Welcomed Me: A Sourcebook on Hospitality in Early Christianity*. Nashville: Abingdon, 2001.

Walzer, Michael. *On Toleration*. New Haven: Yale University Press, 1997.

CHAPTER FOUR

LOVE AND TRUTH IN DEMOCRATIC SOCIETIES: FETHULLAH GÜLEN AND POPE BENEDICT XVI ON SOCIAL QUESTIONS

Thomas Michel

O n June 29, 2009, Pope Benedict XVI issued a new encyclical letter entitled *Caritas in Veritate*, *Love in Truth* or *Truth-Filled Love*. This letter was directed at Christians and to all those who are interested in facing serious questions regarding democracy, justice, and development in our modern world. The influential Muslim scholar Fethullah Gülen has also written extensively on many of these topics. In what follows, I will bring together the views of these two religious leaders in a type of "dialogue of ideas."

In presenting the views of Fethullah Gülen and Pope Benedict XVI on some of the social questions of our time, I do not intend to take a "comparative" approach by simply juxtaposing the ideas of one to those of the other, e.g., "Hoca Effendi says this about democracy, and the Pope says that." Each of these men approaches the issues in his own way, and I propose to let each treat his central concerns as he sees fit. I hope that the flow will reflect that of a scholarly conversation between two intelligent and deeply religious believers, each of whom has exhaustive knowledge of his respective religious heritage and who has given much thought and prayer to the basic human issues that confront us all.

Religion and Democracy

Gülen. In what way can we speak about a particular religion and its relation to democracy? The question is pertinent because many newspaper articles and scholarly papers purport to examine, for example, "Islam and democracy." One reason for the frequency of this approach is that many scholars are willing to treat religion solely as a sociological, economic, or political phenomenon, while denying or ignoring the spiritual, immutable, and trans-rational nature of religious faith. Gülen admits that even some Muslims raise issues about whether Islam and democracy are compatible and asks whether this kind of question is valid or can be productive of truth.

Gülen holds that religion in general and Islam in particular cannot be considered on the same basis with democracy or any other political, social, or economic system. Political, social, and economic systems are by their nature transient and variable. American democracy is not the same as German, Turkish, or French democracy, nor is American democracy today the same phenomenon that it was 40-50 years ago. By its very nature, every political system is subject to limitations of time and space. By contrast, religion deals with eternal, unchanging realities. Religious faith concerns the nature of God, the teaching of the prophets, the message of Scriptures, the existence of angels, and the expectation of Judgment; these are all matters that have nothing to do with changing times and temporary institutions.[1] Religion is concerned with the worship of God and the universal and unchanging standards of morality, which do not depend on changing times and worldly life. Thus, any comparison between religion and democracy or any other political system is bound to limp.

Benedict. In his encyclical, Benedict agrees that it is not the role of religion to propose technical solutions to political or economic problems, nor should religious communities be interfering in the politics of national states. The mission of the Church is, rather, to speak the truth about individuals and societies, about human dignity and the human

---

[1] Fethullah Gülen, *Toward a Global Civilization of Love and Tolerance*, (Somerset: New Jersey: 2006): 345.

vocation. These are principles that are applicable in every political and economic system and remain equally valid at different periods of history. Without this concern for and focus on the truth, according to Pope Benedict, "it would be easy to fall into an empiricist and skeptical view of life, incapable of rising to the level of praxis because of a lack of interest in grasping the values — sometimes even the meanings — with which to judge and direct it."[2]

The point of correspondence between Gülen's thought and that of the Pope lies in the perennial nature of religion in confronting the ever-changing nature of political and economic life. For Benedict, the Church does not engage in problem-solving of technical matters that by their nature are bound up with situations unique to each time and place. Similarly, it is not the task of the Church to interfere in the politics of nations by which the constantly changing daily affairs of citizens are governed. The role of religion is, rather, to ask and raise questions about truth that transcends particular events, systems, and individuals. If people of faith do not continually raise these ageless concerns of truth, we would all be condemned to be governed by spreadsheets, short-term forecasts, public opinion polls, and similar political and economic indicators.

For Gülen, matters of faith transcend the vicissitudes of history and the variations in political systems. Like Benedict, he sees religion as being concerned with the eternal truths of life and existence, what he calls "immutable principles related to faith, worship, and morality." Gülen acknowledges that Islam has worldly aspects, although these come to no more than 5% of the teaching of the prophets. However, these aspects, despite their relative unimportance compared to eternal truths of faith, can be treated in the context of democracy.

The Varieties of Democratic Experience

As noted above, Gülen holds that democracy is not one thing, but is continually developing and constantly producing new variations. It is a system subject to continual development and constant revision. History's

---

[2] Benedict XVI, *Love in Truth (Caritas in Veritate)*, 29 June 2009, par. 9.

first well-documented democracy, that of Athens, was both a *direct* democracy—direct rule by a free assembly of the people—and a *limited* democracy—women and slaves could not participate. Most of our modern states have not adopted the principle of direct democracy, but have opted, rather, for representative democracy, where sovereignty is exercised by elected officials. In a further variation, some countries, like many states of the United States, have what can be called deliberative democracy, which through the mechanisms of initiative, referendum, and recall introduce elements of direct democracy into a basically representative system.

Different democratic countries have combined and adapted these basic democratic functions in various ways. Moreover, in each case, the democratic processes are constantly being subjected to revision and fine-tuning. As elements of the process are found to be functioning poorly or immobilized by constitutional crisis, new refinements are introduced to which the populace gives but a provisional commitment. Otherwise, the system is pragmatically allowed to stand for the time being, always with the awareness that the actual form any democracy takes at any given time is tentative and impermanent.

Gülen. Gülen's view that democracy is a system that is continually being developed and revised is thus a point well taken. One cannot make universal, sweeping statements about democracy and its compatibility with religion without taking into account the tentative and passing nature of all democracies, as well as the variations that occur according to region, culture, and circumstance. Therefore, it is not the role of Islam or any other religion to propose or endorse any unchangeable form of government or to attempt to shape its institutions.[3] What the religion of Islam does is to establish fundamental principles that should orient the general character and standards of a government, while leaving people free to choose the type and form of government most suitable according to the demands of time and circumstances.[4]

---

[3] Gülen, *Toward a Global Civilization of Love and Tolerance*, p. 346.

[4] Fethullah Gülen, "A Comparative Approach to Islam and Democracy," *SAIS (School of Advanced International Studies) Review* 21, no. 2 (2001): 134.

Thus, it is natural and proper for Muslim organizations and movements, just like other members of civil society, to propose principles and values for the consideration of government authorities.

Benedict. We can note the correspondence of these views with those of Benedict XVI in his 2009 encyclical:

> The State does not need to have identical characteristics everywhere. The support aimed at strengthening weak constitutional systems can easily be accompanied by the development of other political players, of a cultural, social, territorial or religious nature, alongside the State. The articulation of political authority at the local, national and international levels is one of the best ways of giving direction to the process of economic globalization. It is also the way to ensure that it does not actually undermine the foundations of democracy.[5]

The Pope is suggesting that political flexibility is needed today in order for governments to control and regulate the complex interactions and often-instantaneous transactions of globalized economics. The improved capabilities of democracies to deal with economic globalization depends on both the increased effectiveness of local, national, and international authority as well as on the simultaneous strengthening of other sectors of civil society, religious, cultural, and regional.

Characteristics of Democratic Societies

Gülen. According to Gülen, in democratic societies, people govern themselves as opposed to being ruled by someone above. Hence, in a democracy, it is the individual that has priority over the community. On the one hand, the just rights and aspirations of the individual must not be stifled by communitarian expediency while, on the other hand, individualism is not an absolute value in itself. In order to live in society, individuals must adjust to realities and limit their own freedoms. This ongoing process of adjustment — balancing the claims of the individual with the demands of the community — is one that is occurring with greater or lesser success in every country today.

---

5   Benedict XVI, Love in Truth (Caritas in Veritate), par. 41.

In applying these standards to his native Turkey, Gülen is optimistic, but he does not shy away from self-criticism. "Democratization is an irreversible process in Turkey," he states in response to those who claim that his movement seeks to overthrow the Turkish Republic.[6] Nevertheless, the democratic ideal still lags behind that of other countries: "Standards of democracy and justice [in Turkey] must be elevated to the level of our contemporaries in the West."[7]

Benedict. For Pope Benedict, the great advantage of democracy, and the reason why he urges Christians to faithfully support this political option, is that of all systems of government, "democracy alone can guarantee equality and rights to everyone."[8] It is the conviction that democracy is that form of government that can best guarantee justice for the most people that recommends it to the Pope. "There is a reciprocal dependence between democracy and justice," he holds, "that impels everyone to work responsibly to safeguard each person's rights, especially those of the weak and marginalized."

It could even be said that the achievement of justice and a dignified life for all, especially the most vulnerable, is one of the main goals of democracy. Benedict holds that "[d]emocracy will attain its full actualization only when every person and each people have access to the primary goods (life, food, water, health care, education, work, and the certainty of their rights) through an ordering of internal and international relations that assures each person of the possibility of participating in them."[9]

Gülen. Gülen arrives at a similar position by applying principles drawn from the Islamic ethical tradition. Starting from the standard of equality enunciated in a hadith from the Prophet Muhammad, Gülen

---

6 Fethullah Gülen, "Interview," *Sabah*, 27 January 1995, cited in "The Gulen Movement: the Turkish Puritans," *Turkish Islam and the Secular State*, (Syracuse, N.Y.: Syracuse U.P., 2003): 28.

7 Fethullah Gülen, "Turkey Assails a Revered Islamic Moderate," *Turkish Daily News*, 25 August 2000.

8 Benedict XVI, "Address to the Italian Christian Workers' Associations (A.C.L.I.)," 27 January 2006.

9 Benedict XVI, "Address to Members of the 'Centesimus Annus' Foundation," 19 May 2006.

holds that no individual, family, or ethnic group has any inherent "right to rule," nor does wealth or power bestow any political privileges. The political ethics taught by Islam can be summed up in six principles:

1. Power derives from truth, not truth from power.
2. Indispensability of justice and rule of law.
3. Individual rights: life, belief, property, reproduction, and health.
4. Privacy and immunity of the individual.
5. No conviction without evidence, no punishment for another's crimes.
6. Administration through consultation.[10]

So long as these principles are followed, Islamic teaching can accept a variety of governmental systems. Muhammad Çetin notes, "According to Gülen the understanding of democracy and human rights within the theoretical heritage of Islam is not dogmatic, but it centers around values such as compromise, stability, the protection of the life, honor and dignity of the human being, justice, equity, dialogue, and consultation."[11] Greg Barton agrees: "Gülen frequently endorses democracy specifically, arguing that it is the most appropriate form of government for the modern period and one that is entirely compatible with Islam."[12] Similarly, while Islamic faith can be lived out in a variety of social and political contexts, the Islamic values that should embody this way of life are those taught in the Qur'an. In this regard, Gülen mentions the primacy of truth or right over force, and the ideals of love, mutual respect, assistance, and social education.[13]

Benedict. For Benedict XVI, the reciprocal link between democracy and justice is oriented toward achieving integral human development

---

[10] Gülen, *Toward a Global Civilization of Love and Tolerance*, 347

[11] Muhammad Çetin, "Fethullah Gülen and the Contribution of Islamic scholarship to Democracy," *The Fountain*, 4 January 2009.

[12] Greg Barton, "Preaching by Example and Learning for Life: Understanding the Gülen Hizmet in the Global Context of Religious Philanthropy and Civil Religion," *Muslim World in Transition: Contributions of the Gulen Movement*, (London: Leeds Metropolitan U.P., 2007): p. 655.

[13] Gülen, *Toward a Global Civilization of Love and Tolerance*, 351

so that all people can live in a way compatible with their human dignity. By "integral human development" he understands "the goal of rescuing peoples, first and foremost, from hunger, deprivation, endemic diseases, and illiteracy. From the economic point of view, this means their active participation, on equal terms, in the international economic process; from the social point of view, it means their evolution into educated societies marked by solidarity; from the political point of view, it means the consolidation of democratic regimes capable of ensuring freedom and peace."[14]

Where the demands of justice are not met, the very functioning of democracy is in danger. The Pope envisions justice as permitting trust, on which all social solidarity depends. He explains:

> Through the systemic increase of social inequality, both within a single country and between the populations of different countries (i.e. the massive increase in relative poverty), not only does social cohesion suffer, thereby placing democracy at risk, but so too does the economy, through the progressive erosion of "social capital" — the network of relationships of trust, dependability, and respect for rules, all of which are indispensable for any form of civil coexistence.[15]

Although they differ in phrasing, there is much in common between Gülen's Islamic vision and the Christian ideal expressed by the Pope. For both, true democracy, which is based on justice and oriented toward the common good of human development, is informed by the values expressed in religious insight. For Gülen, it is the Islamic virtues of truth, love, solidarity, assistance, and mutual respect. For Benedict, it is truth, love, participation, solidarity, and peace.

Religious Freedom

Gülen. According to Gülen, the type of government recommended by Islamic teaching is one based on a social contract between the governors and the governed. The ideal envisioned by the Islamic tradition is

---

[14] Benedict XVI, *Love in Truth (Caritas in Veritate)*, par. 21
[15] Benedict XVI, *Love in Truth*, par. 32

that of a representative system in which the legislators and executives are elected by the people, who establish a majlis or parliament, debate issues, and pass laws in accord with the will of the people. In this way, the society as a whole participates in auditing and holding responsible the administration.[16] Although these are the principles that characterize virtually all the modern democracies, Gülen explains that these principles of governance that are accepted by modern people around the world today are the same as those taught by Islam. Gülen is careful to spell out this compatibility in response to the chorus of critics who continue to ask whether the religion of Islam is compatible with democracy.

For this reason, Gülen emphasizes that these are not simply his own ideas but are, rather, the social values taught by the Islamic tradition itself. He notes that in the time of the first four caliphs, the principles of democracy and free elections were followed. Even when, after the death of Ali, governance of the Islamic umma was transformed from caliphate into a hereditary sultanate, many of the features of modern democracies were still being practiced. He points out, for example, that Jews and Christians enjoyed religious rights under the rule of Islamic governments and that respect for minority rights consistently forms part of the heritage of Islamic values.

Benedict. The importance of religious freedom is one that Gülen shares with Benedict XVI, who emphasized the point when he spoke to the representatives of other religions who gathered to meet him on his trip to Washington, D.C. in April 2008. He pointed out that, in order to protect the rights to religious freedom, particularly of minorities, it is not sufficient to pass laws to prohibit discrimination. Compliance requires vigilance and monitoring on the part of all. He went on:

> The task of upholding religious freedom is never completed. New situations and challenges invite citizens and leaders to reflect on how their decisions respect this basic human right. Protecting religious freedom within the rule of law does not guarantee that peoples — particularly minorities — will be

---

[16] Gülen, *Toward a Global Civilization of Love and Tolerance*, 350

spared unjust forms of discrimination and prejudice. This requires constant effort on the part of all members of society to ensure that citizens are afforded the opportunity to worship peaceably and to pass on their religious heritage to their children.[17]

Similarly, one might say, it is not sufficient for each religious group to defend the rights of its own members (e.g., Christians defending the rights of Christians, Muslims those of Muslims etc.). Rather, everyone has an obligation to defend the right to religious freedom of whatever group is suffering from discrimination or injustice. Moreover, the witness of each religion to the importance of religious freedom as a basic human right will be more credible and powerful if the followers of various religions would come together to defend this right. It is especially incumbent on members of the majority group, which usually have greater access to political and social authorities, to support the just causes of religious minorities, and their willingness to sustain minority rights is a measure of their own credibility.

Democracy and Holistic Development

Gülen. If there is one area in which the thought of Gülen and Benedict XVI most strongly coincide it is the conviction that social systems must address the whole person. According to Gülen, any attempt at treating people solely as *homo economicus* or *homo politicus*, disregarding the spiritual dimension of the human person and the spiritual needs that flow from the immaterial aspects of human nature, is doomed to failure. Gülen is convinced, rather, that if democracy takes a holistic approach to the human person, it can be the instrument for permitting greater opportunities for happiness to the greatest number of people. He makes this eloquent appeal: "If human beings are considered as a whole, without disregarding the spiritual dimension of their existence and their spiritual needs, and without forgetting that human life is not limited to this mortal life and that all people have a great craving for

---

[17] Benedict XVI, "Address to the Representatives of Other Religions," Washington, D.C., 23 April 2008.

eternity, democracy could reach the peak of perfection and bring even more happiness to humanity."[18]

Benedict. In the final section of his encyclical *Caritas in Veritate*, Benedict XVI arrives at a similar position. He affirms that "[d]evelopment must include not just material growth but also spiritual growth," since the human person is a "unity of body and soul," born of God's creative love and destined for eternal life.[19] When a person is far from God, he or she becomes unsettled, and social and psychological alienation sets in. Benedict holds that "the many neuroses that afflict affluent societies are attributable in part to spiritual factors," and new types of slavery in the form of hopelessness and addictions can be explained by economic development and political freedom without corresponding attention to spiritual growth. He concludes: "There cannot be holistic development and universal common good unless people's spiritual and moral welfare is taken into account, considered in their totality as body and soul."[20]

Conclusion: The Contribution of Islamic Humanism and Christian Humanism to Democracy and Development

Because of the essential component of the spiritual to the integral growth of the human person in society, religions such as Islam and Christianity have an indispensable contribution to make to the growth of democracy and human development, just as they have an inescapable responsibility to offer their societies the insights arising from their spiritual experience. As Gülen puts it: "I believe that Islam also would enrich democracy in answering the deep needs of humans, such as spiritual satisfaction, which cannot be fulfilled except through the remembrance of the Eternal One."[21]

---

[18] Gülen, *Toward a Global Civilization of Love and Tolerance*, 352
[19] Benedict XVI, *Love in Truth*, par. 76
[20] Benedict XVI, *Love in Truth*, par. 76
[21] Fethullah Gülen, "'An Interview with Fethullah Gülen,' translated by Zeki Saritoprak and Ali Unal," *The Muslim World, Islam in Contemporary Turkey: The Contribution of Fethullah Gülen* 95, no. 3, (July 2005): p. 452.

If Gülen is calling for "an Islamic humanism" on the part of Muslims, Benedict's conviction that what is needed for genuine development is a "Christian humanism" on the part of Christians. He says: "The greatest service to development is a Christian humanism that enkindles love and takes its lead from truth, accepting both as a lasting gift from God. Ideological rejection of God and an atheism of indifference, oblivious to the Creator and at risk of becoming equally oblivious to human values, constitute some of the chief obstacles to development today. A humanism that excludes God is an inhuman humanism. Only humanism open to the Absolute can guide us in the promotion and building of forms of social and civic life — structures, institutions, culture, and ethos — without exposing us to the risk of becoming ensnared by the fashions of the moment.[22]

Almost 100 years ago, the Muslim scholar Said Nursi called on his students to unite with genuine Christians in opposing atheistic and materialistic tendencies that, according to the teachings of all the prophets, must inevitably result in destructive and self-destructive human behavior. Nursi thought true Muslims and Christians had a common mission to save modern societies from heedless tendencies that cause human misery. I believe that in our day, these two thinkers — Fethullah Gülen and Pope Benedict XVI, one Muslim and the other Christian — can give us a sound conceptual basis on which we can discuss, in truth and love, the contribution that, by our obedience to God, we can offer together to our modern societies.

Works Cited

Barton, Greg. "Preaching by Example and Learning for Life: Understanding the Gülen Hizmet in the Global Context of Religious Philanthropy and Civil Religion." *Muslim World in Transition: Contributions of the Gulen Movement.* London: Leeds Metropolitan U.P. (2007): 655.

Benedict XVI. "Address to Members of the 'Centesimus Annus' Foundation." 19 May 2006.

Benedict XVI. "Address to the Italian Christian Workers' Associations (A.C.L.I.)." 27 January 2006.

---

22 Benedict XVI, *Love in Truth*, par. 78

Benedict XVI. "Address to the Representatives of Other Religions." Washington, D.C., 23 April 2008.

Benedict XVI. *Love in Truth (Caritas in Veritate)*, 29 June 2009.

Çetin, Muhammad. "Fethullah Gülen and the Contribution of Islamic scholarship to Democracy." *The Fountain.* 4 January 2009.

Gülen, Fethullah. "A Comparative Approach to Islam and Democracy." SAIS (School of Advanced International Studies) Review, 21, 2 (2001): 134.

Gülen, Fethullah. "'An Interview with Fethullah Gülen,' translated by Zeki Saritoprak and Ali Unal." *The Muslim World, Islam in Contemporary Turkey: The Contribution of Fethullah Gülen* 95, no. 3 (July 2005): 452.

Gülen, Fethullah. "Interview." *Sabah.* 27 January 1995. Cited in "The Gulen Movement: the Turkish Puritans." *Turkish Islam and the Secular State.* Syracuse, N.Y.: Syracuse U.P., (2003): p. 28.

Gülen, Fethullah. *Toward a Global Civilization of Love and Tolerance.* Somerset, New Jersey: 2006.

Gülen, Fethullah. "Turkey Assails a Revered Islamic Moderate." *Turkish Daily News.* 25 August 2000.

CHAPTER FIVE

MUSLIM CHRISTIAN DIALOGUE: NOSTRA AETATE AND FETHULLAH GÜLEN'S VISION

Salih Yucel

Introduction[1]

At a time when half of the Ottoman Empire's lands were occupied by Russia, Italy, England, and France, Said Nursi proposed dialogue and collaboration between Muslims and Christians before a congregation of over 10,000 Muslims, including 100 prominent religious scholars, in the Umayyad Mosque, Damascus.[2] The strength of Nursi's proposal comes from his foresight when other Muslim thinkers were on the defensive against the invading colonial forces. Nursi held this approach even after the Ottoman Empire had collapsed after a turbulent conflict between the Empire and Europe.

Nursi strongly believed that the source of international aggression is materialistic philosophy. The problem was not East vs. West or Christian vs. Muslim, but the philosophy that he regarded as "the evil of civilization." For Nursi, there are two types of Europe: "the first follows the sciences which serve justice and activities beneficial for the

---

[1] This article first appeared in the *Australian eJournal of Theology*, 20.3 (December 2013). Used with permission.

[2] Said Nursi, *Hutbe-i Şâmiye (Damascus Sermon),* translated from Turkish by Şükran Vahide (Istanbul: Sözler Publication, 1996), 18.

life of society through the inspiration it has received from true Christianity." The second is "corrupt, through the darkness of the philosophy of naturalism...which has driven humankind to vice and misguidance."[3] This philosophy drives people to greed, which then causes major conflicts from individual to global levels.

This was the reasoning behind his call for unity and collaboration between followers of the two major faiths, Muslims and Christians. Both have common enemies, such as the problems of poverty, ignorance, and enmity. "Believers should now unite, not only with their Muslim fellow-believers, but with truly religious and pious Christians, disregarding questions of dispute and not arguing over them, for absolute disbelief is on the attack."[4] Nursi faced imprisonment, political exile, and home arrest during the second half of his life, making him unable to put his vision in practice.

It was over half-a-century after Nursi's proposal that the Second Vatican Council declared *Nostra Aetate*, "The Relation of the Church to Non-Christian Religions" in 1965. The declaration was originally intended to deal with the Catholic theological standing towards Judaism. It was not until Arab Catholic, Maronite, and Coptic bishops argued that a statement which ignored Muslims was not politically viable that Muslims were included in the declaration.[5] *Nostra Aetate* is a significant document that challenges Roman Catholics as well as Protestant Churches to open up, rethink their attitudes towards other religions, and reflect on the fact that all human beings are "but one community."[6]

---

3   Said Nursi, *Lemalar (The Flashes)*, translated from Turkish by Sukran Vahide, (Istanbul: Sozler Publications 1996), 161.

4   Nursi, *Lemalar*, 204.

5   Kail Ellis, O.S.A, "Vatican II and the Contemporary Islam," *New Catholic World*, 23, no. 1386 (Nov/Dec. 1988), 269ff; Edward Idris Cardinal Cassidy, *Ecumenism and Interreligious Dialogue: Unitatis Redintegratio, Nostra Aetate* (New York: Paulist Press, 2005), 127.

6   Ataullah Siddiqui, *Christian-Muslim Dialogue in the Twentieth Century* (London: Macmillan Press, 1997), 34.

Nostra Aetate has been considered one of the most important turning points in the history of Catholic-Muslim relations.[7] In the words of Pope Benedict XVI in 2005, *Nostra Aetate* is the *Magna Carta* of the Catholic Church in terms of Muslim-Christian relations.[8] Since 1967, the popes have congratulated Muslims on Eid al-Fitr after the month of Ramadan. In 1974, the Vatican formed the Commission for Religious Relations with Muslims (CRRM). In 1976, the Vatican co-organized the Christian-Islam Congress in Tripoli with the World Islamic Call Society (WICS). In 1990, the Vatican established the *Nostra Aetate* Foundation. In 1994, the Pontifical Council for Interreligious Dialogue (PCID) led a conference with the Muslim World League, the Organisation of the Islamic Conference, and the Muslim World Congress in Cairo. In 1995, the Muslim-Christian Liaison Committee was set up with four international Muslim organizations. The Permanent Committee for Dialogue set up a joint committee with Al-Azhar University's Monotheist Religions Committee in 1998 with the signing of an agreement in Rome.

In 2001, the previous Pope, John Paul II, visited the Umayyad Mosque as the first pope to visit a mosque, 1,363 years after Caliph 'Umar ibn Khattab (586-644) who visited the Church of the Holy Sepulchre in Jerusalem. 2007 was the year 138 Muslim scholars and leaders signed an open letter called "A Common Word between Us and You" to Pope Benedict XVI as a response to the Pope's remarks at the University of Regensburg lecture. In 2008, the PCID and the Centre for Interreligious Dialogue of the Islamic Culture and Relations Organisation made a joint declaration in Iran. Last February, the Vatican and al-Azhar University's Joint Committee for Dialogue signed a declaration promoting a culture of peace. In Catholic archdioceses in many coun-

---

[7] Scott C. Alexander, "We Go Way Back: The History of Muslim-Catholic Relations Is One of Both Confrontation and Dialogue." *U.S. Catholic* (February 2007).

[8] John Borelli, "*Interreligious Dialogue as a Spiritual Practice*," Georgetown University international conference proceedings, *Islam in the Age of Global Challenges: Alternative Perspectives of the Gulen Movement Conference*. Available at http://en.fgulen.com/conference-papers/gulen-conference-in-washington-dc/3100-interreligious-dialogue-as-a-spiritual-practice

tries, there is a committee devoted to interfaith relations. These are all fruits of the *Nostra Aetate* declaration.

Gülen's Approach

Both Said Nursi and Fethullah Gülen were aware that the theology of dialogue between Christians and Muslims precedes this declaration by centuries. Dialogue between the two communities, in fact, goes back to the beginning of Islam, and the Qur'an itself invites Christians to dialogue *with fair words* in order to adore the one God (Qur'an 3:64) and invites Muslims to converse with Christians in a courteous manner.[9] (Qur'an 26:46)[10] However, this fact, together with historical and current Muslim-initiated dialogue activities is not as well publicized as *Nostra Aetate* due to the lack of a religious hierarchy in Islam. Therefore, Muslim leaders attempt to "offer authoritative statements based on scholarly and sectarian credentials."[11]

Leading Muslim thinker and the spiritual leader of a global movement, Fethullah Gülen, studied Nursi's approach to other religions, specifically Christianity, and applied Nursi's philosophy beyond *Nostra Aetate*. In 1986, Gülen asked his followers to engage in dialogue with people from all the diverse segments of Turkish society, from the left to the right wing, and the secular to the agnostic or atheist. He inspired his followers to establish the Journalists' and Writers' Foundation in 1994 and other dialogue centres with this aim,[12] thereby becoming the first

---

[9]   Khaled Akasheh, "Nostra Ateate: 40 Years Later," *L'Osservatore Romano* (Weekly Edition in English), (28 June 2006), 8.

[10] "And do not argue with the People of the Scripture except in a way that is best..." (Qur'an 26:49).

[11] Turan Kayaoglu, *Preachers of Dialogue: International Relations and Interfaith Theology*, international conference proceedings, *Muslim World in Transition: Contributions of the Gülen Movement*, (Leeds: Leeds Metropolitan University Press, 2007), 521.

[12] In the US alone, there are over 50 interfaith dialogue centres whose establishment was inspired by Gülen. Thomas Michel, SJ, *"Fighting Poverty with Kimse Yok Mu?"* Georgetown University international conference proceedings, *Islam in the Age of Global Challenges: Alternative Perspectives of the Gulen Movement Conference.* (Now it is more than 200 throughout the world).

leading person behind the institutionalization of dialogue in the Turkish context.

Gülen has been called "one of the most persuasive and influential voices in the Muslim community" calling for dialogue.[13] Gülen regards interfaith cooperation as "compulsory for Muslims to support peace"[14] relying on the basic Islamic sources to affirm this point.[15] Enes Ergene, a pupil of Gülen's study circle, writes that Gülen does not rely on theological sources alone. "These two concepts [tolerance and dialogue], first developed on a small scale, have turned into a search for a culture of reconciliation on a world scale.... Gülen strengthens this search with religious, legal, and philosophical foundations."[16] In his view, a human being is related to everything in the cosmos; to engage in dialogue with other related beings is therefore part of human nature.

Another of Gülen's students, Mehmet Seker, posits that Gülen has two aims for interfaith and intercultural dialogue. Firstly, he seeks a world in which civilisations do not clash. Secondly, he pictures a world where religious, cultural and linguistic differences are not denied or repressed, but rather expressed freely in the form of a civilisation of love. He dreams of a world without conflict and enmity. In such a world, people avoid hurting or annoying each other.[17]

From the establishment of the Republic of Turkey up until around 1990, the meeting of Muslim and non-Muslim leaders was considered unacceptable. However, Gülen broke this unwritten rule and met with

---

13   Thomas Michel, SJ, "*Two Frontrunners for Peace: John Paul II and Fethullah Gulen,*" http://en.fgulen.com/content/view/1944/13/, accessed May, 19, 2009.

14   Zeki Saritoprak, "An Islamic Approach to Peace and Nonviolence: A Turkish Experience," *The Muslim World,* 95 (July 2005), 423.

15   Ismail Albayrak, "The Juxtaposition of Islam and Violence" in Hunt and Aslandogan, op cit., 127; and M. Hakan Yavuz, *The Gulen Movement: The Turkish Puritans*" in M.Hakan Yavuz & John L. Esposito, *Turkish Islam and The Secular State. The Gülen Movement.* (New York Syracuse University Press, 2003), 19-47.

16   Enes Ergene, *The Gulen Movement, Dialogue, and Tolerance,* 5 Aug 2008, http://www.fethullahgulen.org/about-fethullah-gulen/an-analysis-of-the-gulen-movement/3022-the-gulen-movement-dialogue-and-tolerance.html, accessed May 20, 2009.

17   Mehmet Seker, *Musbet Hareket* (Istanbul: Isik Yayinlari, 2006), 80.

the Chief Rabbi of Turkey David Pinto, the Armenian Patriarch Mesrob Mutafyan, Sephardic Chief Rabbi of Jerusalem Eliyahu Bakshi-Doron, Christian Orthodox Patriarch Bartholomeos in Istanbul, and former Vatican Representative Monsignor George Marowich, who then arranged Gülen's meeting with Pope John Paul II at the Vatican in 1998. During his meeting with the Pope, Gülen proposed the establishment of a joint school of Divinity in Urfa, Turkey, the birthplace of Abraham, to disprove the idea of "a clash of civilizations."[18] While such meetings may be welcomed today, it was almost taboo during the 1990s in the political and religious atmosphere in Turkey. The meetings, especially with the Pope, were harshly criticized by ultra-secularists and some Islamists. A group of young Islamists argued that Gülen should not have humiliated himself to the extent of going to the Vatican and meeting with the Pope. Gülen, however, responded to this kind of reductionism by saying that humility was an attribute of Muslims.[19]

In 1999, Gülen travelled to the US to seek medical attention, and remained there due to the political conditions in Turkey. His followers in the US have been active in realizing his vision, especially after 9/11. With his encouragement, over 50 dialogue centres were established in North America by his followers and supporters. Although no official count has taken place, it is possible that the number exceeds 100 in the Americas, Europe, and Australia. Other Muslim organizations or groups have put effort into interfaith relations, but Gülen's followers and sup-porters have actually established dialogue centres, and have given more time, funds, and efforts to this sector.

One reason for the success of the Gülen Movement (also known as the Hizmet Movement in Western countries) is the universal nature of

---

[18] Loye Ashton & Tamer Balci, *A Contextual Analysis of the Supporters and Critics of the Gülen/Hizmet Movement*, Georgetown University international conference proceedings, *Islam in the Age of Global Challenges: Alternative Perspectives of the Gülen Movement Conference*, 84, available at http://en.fgulen.com/conference-papers/gulen-conference-in-washington-dc/3123-a-contextual-analysis-of-the-supporters-and-critics-of-the-gulen-movement

[19] Zeki Saritoprak & Sidney Grifith, "Fethullah Gülen and the 'People of the Book': A Voice from Turkey for Interfaith Dialogue," *The Muslim World*, 95, no. 3 (2005), 329-341.

Gülen's vision, exemplified by his nonviolent and tolerant approach during a time marked by fear of religious extremism. Based on personal examination of some of these centre's activities via the Internet[20], it is evident that these dialogue centres do not engage with the religious segment alone. Besides the usual dialogue activities such as dinners, seminars, and conferences, these centres organize joint projects, such as food drives, interfaith education curriculum design, and trips to holy sites in Istanbul, Jerusalem, Rome, and London. They have entered the academic sector and published articles, magazines, and books. Through high school and university student exchange programs, these centres are reaching out to the younger demographic in order to achieve their aim of the cultural acceptance of dialogue.

Over the course of time, the activities of the Movement eventually gained more attention through public relations works and general publicity. It attracted the attention of the academic world which slowly began studying its global projects and productions. After some years of study, Gülen's followers and admirers, both Muslim and non-Muslim, founded tertiary institutes devoted to the study and research of interfaith relations, faith, and spirituality. Among these are the Nursi Chair in Islamic Studies at John Carroll University in Ohio, the Fethullah Gülen Chair in the Study of Islam and Muslim-Catholic Relations at the Australian Catholic University in Melbourne, Australia, the Fethullah Gülen Chair at Syarif Hidayetullah Islam University, Indonesia, Gülen Institute at Houston University and Fethullah Gülen Chair for Intercultural Studies at Catholic University of Leuven in Belgium.

Institutionalising of Dialogue

In *Christian-Muslim Dialogue in the Twentieth Century*, Ataullah Siddiqui analyses the definitions and methods of prominent Muslim scholars in the case of interfaith dialogue. Dialogue is understood as meeting and communicating with other faiths, sharing thoughts and exchanging

---

[20] Some of these websites : http://www.interfaithdialog.org, www.idcnj.org, http://www.interfaithdialog.org/ http://www.guleninstitute.org/, http://www.intercultural.org.au/,

views, and reaching mutual understanding and respect through focusing on common ground.[21]

However, Nursi and Gülen go beyond this understanding of dialogue. Interfaith dialogue needs to be institutionalized and collaboration must take place through joint projects for there to be any effectual dialogue in the current atmosphere of scepticism. Dialogue programs occur at a local level with small projects on the part of other Muslim organizations, but larger-scale programs and projects that attract public attention are needed.[22]

It is for this purpose that during his meeting with the Pope, Gülen proposed the establishment of a joint divinity school, student exchange programs between divinity schools, and joint trips to holy sites. There was no response from the Vatican, possibly due to political conditions in Turkey. If this project had become a reality, it would have been a first and original institution, serving as a model in the world.

The silence from the Vatican did not discourage Gülen since he was aiming for more than a Turkey-Vatican dialogue. When Samuel Huntington's wrote about "the clash of civilizations," Gülen put forth his ideas on the cooperation of civilizations. Gülen is working for an inter-civilizational dialogue,[23] one that transgresses beyond religious identity. This point is another significant difference in Gülen's understanding of current dialogue activities. He bases dialogue not entirely on the grounds of faith, but on *muhabbet*, love. Gülen's social philosophy revolves around the idea of serving humanity, and institutions should serve this purpose. Institutes formed by one group will not be all-embracing, but those formed by a coalition of groups, such as interfaith groups, will serve a greater population.

Analysis and Criticism

Nostra Aetate was the first step in promoting the culture of dialogue with Muslims. Despite the mention of shared values between the two faiths and the urge to promote social justice and moral welfare, there

---

[21] Siddiqui, *Christian-Muslim Dialogue*, 163-169.

[22] Mahmoud Ayoub, "Christian-Muslim Dialogue: Goals and Obstacles," *The Muslim World*, 94, no. 3 (2004), 313-320.

[23] Saritoprak, & Grifith, *Fethullah Gülen*, 329-341.

are no specifics in terms of collaboration and institutionalization. Most of the joint declarations and committees with Muslims after *Nostra Aetate* could not bring interfaith collaboration into institutionalized dialogue with other Muslim groups apart from the Hizmet Movement. However, it is observed that all Muslim-Christian dialogue has so far achieved is the recognition of the Abrahamic roots of the two faiths.[24]

Not all Muslims and Christians embraced the declaration of *Nostra Aetate*. In 1970, evangelicals convened in Frankfurt, Germany, and signed a declaration called the *Frankfurt Declaration*, underlining the mission of Christ, and harshly criticizing organized dialogue as a "betrayal of the universality of Christ."[25] In both the *Dialogue and Mission* statement by the Secretariat for non-Christians in the Vatican in 1984 and in *Dialogue and Proclamation* in 1991, dialogue is placed within the mission of the Church, the building of God's kingdom,[26] thereby evoking apprehension on the part of Muslims.

Nonetheless, it should be stated that Muslim thinkers often brought polemics to the table, asking that they be resolved before genuine dialogue takes place. In his response to Pope Paul VI's letter regarding Peace Day, Abu 'Ala Mawdudi (1903-1979), founder of the Islamic revivalist party in Pakistan, Jamaat al-Islami, asked that the Pope use all his influence to remove that which poisons the relations between the two faith groups, such as the attacks on Prophet Muhammad and the Qur'an made by Christian scholars. When the Second Vatican Council was discussing the idea of forgetting the historical troubles between Muslims and Christians, French-Indian Muslim leader Professor Muhammad Hamidullah in France responded with a letter to the Pope, requesting that the Vatican officially disavow the Church's past unjustifiable and anti-Islamic resolutions of Councils and Synods. One view-

---

[24] Liyakatali Takim, "From Conversion to Conversation: Interfaith Dialogue in Post 9-11 America," *The Muslim World*, 94, no. 3 (2004), 343-357.

[25] Yvonne Haddad & Wadi Haddad, *Christian-Muslim Encounters* (Gensville: University Press of Florida, 1995), xiii.

[26] Edward Idris Cardinal Cassidy, *Ecumenism and Interreligious Dialogue: Unitatis Redintegratio, Nostra Aetate* (New York: Paulist Press, 2005), 148-150.

point among Muslim thinkers is that forgetting the past is "a way of getting us to disarm ourselves."[27]

Other major thinkers, such as Isma'il Raji al-Faruqi (1921-1986), Mahmoud Ayoub, Hasan Askari, Khurshid Ahmad, Mohammed Talbi, and many other Muslim scholars, placed some conditions before dialogue. There was scepticism regarding dialogue, and fear that it would be used as a missionary tool and carried political agendas. Khurshid Ahmad posited that the West did not view Islam as a religion or civilization, but "merely as a rival political power,"[28] thus making dialogue unbalanced. In the basket was the general mistrust of Muslims due to the negative reputation of missionaries in Muslim lands and the double-standards of the West. For example, Ahmad points out how the West accepts everything from the "bikini to the evening dress" as natural, but sees the *hijab* (head scarf) as unnatural and threatening local culture. In 2005, the rector of Al-Azhar University, the most prestigious religious institution in Sunni Islam, asked the Vatican to ap"ologise for the Crusades.[29]

Looking at the most prominent Muslim leaders and thinkers of the 20th century, we see Said Nursi and Fethullah Gülen, each of whom put sincere interfaith dialogue and collaboration at the forefront, along with the condition of leaving polemics behind and focusing on common points.[30] For Nursi and Gülen to come out with the request for unconditional dialogue is remarkable and bold. If dialogue is institutionalized, it is possible that it will thereby reduce mistrust and criticism.

---

27 Siddiqui, *Christian-Muslim Dialogue,* 55.
28 Ismail R. Al-Faruqi, "Common Bases between the Two Religions in Regard to Convictions, and Points of Agreement in the Spheres of Life," *Seminar of the Islamic-Christian Dialogue* (1976); Tripoli: Popular Office of Foreign Relations, Socialist Peoples Libyan Arab Jamhariya (1981), 243, as cited in Ataullah Siddiqui, *Christian-Muslim Dialogue in the Twentieth Century,* (London: Macmillan Press, 1997), 130.
29 Robert Spencer, "A Vatican Apology for the Crusades?" www.frontpagemagazine.com, March 22, 2005.
30 Fethullah Gülen, *Essays, Perspectives, Opinion* (Rutherford, NJ: The Light Publication, 2002), 34.

The establishment of many interfaith dialogue and cultural centres and academic institutes created scepticism and received criticism in Turkey and abroad. Some opponents accuse the Gülen Movement of concealing a political agenda to change Turkey as a secular republic while others see the Movement as an American project to use soft Islam to control the Muslim world. These opponents range from the ultra-nationalists, radical political Islamists, and ideological leftists in Turkey and some Evangelists and neo-conservatives in the US and around the world.

According to Paul Stenhouse, Gülen seems to be promoting tolerance, understanding, peace and interfaith dialogue, but in reality, he is secretly establishing a caliphate. On the establishment of the Fethullah Gülen Chair of Islamic Studies and Interfaith Dialogue, within the Centre of Inter-Religious Dialogue at the Australian Catholic University in Melbourne, Stenhouse raised questions about Gülen, and implied that the Gülen Movement is a "group that is ex professo dedicated to promoting an Islamist ideology."[31]

However Greg Barton[32] and David Tittensor[33] have dismissed these claims. Reporting in *The Australian* newspaper, Barton dismissed Stenhouse's article as "not particularly well argued" and further stated, "Father Stenhouse conflates this quiescent Sufism with some of the rare examples of Sufi militantism".

Former Vatican Representative in Istanbul Monsignor George Marowich, who has known Gülen for over a decade, bears a special

---

[31] Dogan Koc, "Strategic Defamation of Fethullah Gülen- English Vs Turkish," *European Journal of Economic and Political Studies*, 4, no. 1 (2011), 189-244.

[32] Jill Rowbotham, "Catholic Hits Islamic Chair," *The Australian* (16 January 2008) http://www.theaustralian.com.au/higher-education/catholic-hits-islamic-chair/story-e6frgcjx-1111115325 accessed on July 23, 2013.

[33] David Tittensor, "The Gülen Movement and the Case of a Secret Agenda: Putting the Debate in Perspective," *Journal of Islam and Christian-Muslim Relations*, 23, no. 2 (2012), 163-179.

admiration toward Gülen for his pioneering efforts in dialogue. "He is the Mevlana (Rumi)[34] of our age," he would say.[35]

While Gülen is accused of being Islam's Trojan horse in the Western Christian World, in the Turkish world, he is paradoxically accused of being the Pope's Trojan Horse.[36] Gülen and his followers have also been accused of being "bad representatives" of Islam, and "cater(ing) to" Jews and Christians.[37] Mehmet Sevket Eygi, syndicated columnist for *Milli Gazete,* a publication aligned to former Prime Minister Necmettin Erbakan's Welfare Party, questioned Gülen and his followers on their dialogue activities and representation of Muslims. He did not approve of the activities as it opened the doors to missionaries, and went as far as calling interfaith dialogue un-Islamic and unlawful based on religious texts.

Despite such accusations, Gülen's continuation of dialogue is admirable. In his message at the Parliament of the World's Religions Gülen wrote that dialogue with the adherents of other religious traditions is an integral part of an Islamic ethic that has been long neglected. [38]

---

34 Mevlana Jalal ad-Din Muhammad (1207-1273) was a Persian poet, mystic and theologian who is known in the Western world as Rumi and is revered for his spiritual legacy in Iran, Turkey, Afghanistan and South Asia. The themes in his works transcended national borders with universal values of love, tolerance, compassion and spiritual ecstasy. His works have been translated into many languages. He has been described as the "most popular poet in America." Charles Haviland, "The Roar of Rumi, 800 Years On," *BBC* (30 September 2007), http://news.bbc.co.uk/2/hi/south_asia/7016090.stm.

35 Claims *and Answers,* http://en.fgulen.com/press-room/columns/3280-a-lonely-man-in-a-rest-home, acessed July 21, 2013.

36 Koc, *Strategic Defamation of Fethullah Gülen,* 189-244.

37 This was by two opponents, Haydar Bas, Turkish academic, leader of a small religious community, and politician associated with the Independent Turkey Party (BTP), and SevkiYilmaz, former parliamentary representative of former Prime MinisterNecmettin Erbakan's Welfare Party in Turkey. In Loye Ashton & Tamer Balci, *A Contextual Analysis of the Supporters and Critics of the Gülen/Hizmet Movement,* Georgetown University international conference proceedings, *Islam in the Age of Global Challenges: Alternative Perspectives of the Gülen Movement Conference,* 105.

38 Fethullah Gülen, *The Necessity of Dialogue,* http://www.fethullahgulen.org/about-fethullah-gulen/messages/972-the-necessity-of-interfaith-dialogue-a-muslim-approach.html accessed January 6, 2009.

Seker argues that Gülen's dialogue work is not unislamic or something new to Islam, but is rather based on the the spirit of the *Medina Charter*, an agreement drawn up between the Muslims and non-Muslims (Jews and pagans) in Medina that granted rights and respect towards non-Muslims. Seker adds that Gülen also draws from the spirit of the final sermon of Prophet Muhammad. [39]

The important issue these criticisms raise is one that fails to receive enough attention: that there is no body or institution representing Muslims all over the world, nor is there any agreement on who should represent the adherents of this faith.[40] Interfaith dialogue by Muslims is carried out by government-appointed scholars who are limited in their approaches, leaders of spiritual groups, or small groups and individuals.[41] This makes it difficult for Christians, because it leaves them to engage in dialogue with a variety of Muslim nations, institutions, groups, and spiritual leaders. Moreover this draws criticism from Muslims who feel that the Christian world is not engaging with the right organization or person. In order to overcome this missing link of representation, Muslims and Christians need to establish joint institutions and social welfare organizations.

In 1993, Pope John Paul II in Rome appealed for peace in Bosnia-Herzegovina and called for a special prayer day at Assisi. Forty two delegates, including two Bosnian Muslims, attended the prayer service for Christian, Jewish, and Muslim participants.[42] It is possible that this and similar services inspired cooperation in 1996 when a group of Catholic and Muslim religious people met to discuss how they could support the building of a new water system that would serve both the Muslim community in Fojnica and the Croatian community of Kiseljak, two cities that experienced major violence during the Muslim-Croat fighting in 1993-1994. However, due to lack of local personnel and expertise to

---

[39] Seker, *Musbet Hareket*, 83.
[40] Haddad, Yvonne & Haddad, Wadi, *Christian-Muslim Encounters*, xv.
[41] Siddiqui, *Christian-Muslim Dialogue*, 52.
[42] Cassidi, *Ecumenism and Interreligious Dialogue*, 142.

supervise volunteers, this project was never realized, despite the genuine interest and efforts of local clergy.[43]

Conclusion

We have yet to witness another prominent Muslim leader pronouncing dialogue as an "obligation" apart from Gülen, who holds that dialogue is the duty of Muslims in the struggle to make our world a more peaceful place.[44] Gülen believes that dialogue is among the duties of Muslims on earth because of what it contributes to the promotion of peace and safety in our world.

Both the declaration of *Nostra Aetate* and the vision of Gülen have pushed religious persons to open their doors to each other. Yet, it is only when theories and ideas are applied that they gain credibility and give benefit. Interfaith dialogue faces boundaries of mistrust and scepticism, especially among radical religious people, due to historical relations between the East and West, a lack of credibility and results, and political imbalance between the two sides.

Nostra Aetate was a commendable step. Yet, it was declared over 48 years ago. Vatican and Muslim organizations need to take steps in order to remove the perception of interfaith dialogue as a twentieth-century fashion [45] and "a clubby brotherhood."[46] For any Vatican or Christian initiatives to be successful, Muslim leaders and participants in dialogue need to leave behind historical grudges when engaging in dialogue, even if they do not wish to forget the past. Both Christians and Muslims are equal partners, and not opponents, in dialogue. In addition, the issue of representation on behalf of Muslims must be addressed,

---

43 David Steele, *Contributions of Interfaith Dialogue to Peace building* in the Former Yugoslavia in Interfaith Dialogue and Peace building, ed. David R. Smock (Washington DC: United States Institute of Peace Press, 2002), 85.

44 Zeki Saritoprak & Grifith, *Fethullah Gülen*, 329-341.

45 John Borelli, *Interreligious Dialogue as a Spiritual Practice*, Georgetown University international conference proceedings, *Islam in the Age of Global Challenges: Alternative Perspectives of the Gülen Movement Conference*, 147.

46 Thomas Michel, SJ, *Toward a Dialogue of Liberation with Muslims*, http://www.sjweb.info/dialogo/index.cfm, accessed 20 May, 2009.

possibly by forming a pluralist council where members are democrati-cally elected, representing every nation of the *Ummah*, the Muslim com-munity. While this may not be applicable in current global political, social, and religious conditions in the Muslim world, it is a feasible pos-sibility that could be politically and culturally accepted.

In order to clear the air of hidden agendas, leaders on both sides of the dialogue need to undertake theological reasoning to reduce the concept of the "dialogue mission" and "dialogue *da'wa*"- that is, the use of dialogue for covert proselytism. While it is not possible to complete-ly erase concealed intentions, whether they may be religious, political, or cultural, it is necessary to decrease these and continue the dialogue by focusing on and building from common ground. For Muslims, engag-ing in dialogue evokes hope and arouses fear at the same time.[47] This needs further study in order to understand the roots of this issue.

Institution-oriented dialogue grants opportunities for adherents of different faiths to see the world and each other from different windows. This is one aim and meaning of dialogue: creating a common base to combat materialistic philosophy and aggressive secularism, and work-ing together for social welfare and justice projects. The more this is implemented beyond declarations and discussions, the greater will be its cultural acceptance. This move to institutionalizing dialogue will gain trust once the joint projects produce visible and measurable results that go beyond the common desire for peace. The goal of inter-faith dialogue and collaboration between different peoples is the explo-ration of new dynamics that will benefit all humanity.

References

Akasheh, Khaled. "Nostra Ateate: 40 Years Later." *L'Osservatore Romano*. Weekly Edition in English (28 June 2006): 8.

Albayrak, Ismail. "The Juxtaposition of Islam and Violence." On *Hunt and Aslando-gan*.

Alexander, Scott C. "We Go Way Back: The History of Muslim-Catholic Relations Is One of Both Confrontation and Dialogue." *U.S. Catholic* (February 2007)

---

[47] Haddad & Haddad, *Christian-Muslim Encounters*, xiv.

Al-Faruqi, Isma'il R. "Common Bases between the Two Religions in Regard to Convictions, and Points of Agreement in the Spheres of Life." *Seminar of the Islamic-Christian Dialogue.* Tripoli: Popular Office of Foreign Relations, Socialist Peoples Libyan Arab Jamhariya (1981): 243.

Ashton, Loye & Tamer Balci. "A Contextual Analysis of the Supporters and Critics of the Gülen/Hizmet Movement." Georgetown University International Conference Proceedings. *Islam in the Age of Global Challenges: Alternative Perspectives of the Gülen Movement Conference,* 84.

Ayoub, Mahmoud. "Christian-Muslim Dialogue: Goals and Obstacles." *The Muslim World,* 94, no. 3 (Hartford: July 2004): 313-320.

Bas, Haydar, and Sevki Yilmaz. "Loye Ashton & Tamer Balci, A Contextual Analysis of the Supporters and Critics of the Gülen/Hizmet Movement." Georgetown University International Conference Proceedings. *Islam in the Age of Global Challenges: Alternative Perspectives of the Gülen Movement Conference.*

Borelli, John. "Interreligious Dialogue as a Spiritual Practice." Georgetown University International Conference Proceedings. *Islam in the Age of Global Challenges: Alternative Perspectives of the Gülen Movement Conference.*

Cassidy, Edward Idris Cardinal. "Ecumenism and Interreligious Dialogue: Unitatis Redintegratio." *Nostra Aetate.* New York: Paulist Press, 2005.

Ellis, Kail. O.S.A. "Vatican II and the Contemporary Islam." *New Catholic World,* 23, no. 1386 (Nov/Dec. 1988).

Ergene, Enes. *The Gülen Movement, Dialogue, and Tolerance* (5 Aug. 2008). http://www.fethullahgulen.org/about-fethullah-gulen/an-analysis-of-the-gulen-moveent/3022-the-gulen-movement-dialogue-and-tolerance.html. Gülen, Fethullah. *Essays, Perspectives, Opinion.* Rutherford, NJ: The Light Publication, 2002.

Haddad, Yvonne & Wadi Haddad. *Christian-Muslim Encounters.* University Press of Florida. (1995).

Kayaoglu, Turan. "Preachers of Dialogue: International Relations and Interfaith Theology." International Conference Proceedings. *Muslim World in Transition: Contributions of the Gülen Movement.* Leeds Metropolitan University Press. (2007).

Michel, Thomas SJ. "Fighting Poverty with Kimse Yok Mu?" Georgetown University International Conference Proceedings. *Islam in the Age of Global Challenges: Alternative Perspectives of the Gülen Movement Conference.*

Michel, Thomas SJ. "Two Frontrunners for Peace: John Paul II and Fethullah Gülen." http://en.fgulen.com/content/view/1944/13/.

Michel, Thomas SJ. *Toward a Dialogue of Liberation with Muslims,* http://www.sjweb.info/dialogo/index.cfm.

Nursi, Said. *Hutbe-i Şâmiye* (Damascus Sermon). Translated from Turkish by Şükran Vahide. Istanbul: Sözler Publication, 1996.

Nursi, Said, *Lem'alar* (The Flashes). Translated from Turkish by Sukran Vahide. Istanbul. (1996).

Saritoprak, Zeki. "An Islamic Approach to Peace and Nonviolence: A Turkish Experience." *The Muslim World*, 95 (July 2005).

Saritoprak, Zeki & Sidney Griffith. "Fethullah Gülen and the 'People of the Book:' A Voice from Turkey for Interfaith Dialogue." *The Muslim World*, 95, no. 3. Hartford. (July 2005).

Siddiqui, Ataullah. *Christian-Muslim Dialogue in the 20th Century*. London: Macmillan Press, 1997.

Spencer, Robert. "A Vatican Apology for the Crusades?" *Front Page Magazine*. (22 March 2005).

Steele, David. *Contributions of Interfaith Dialogue to Peacebuilding in the Former Yugoslavia in Interfaith Dialogue and Peacebuilding*. Edited by David R. Smock. Washington DC: United States Institute of Peace Press. (2002).

Takim, Liyakatali. "From Conversion to Conversation: Interfaith Dialogue in Post 9/11 America." *The Muslim World*, 94, no. 3. Hartford. (July 2004): 343-357.

Yavuz, M. Hakan. "The Gülen Movement: The Turkish Puritans." *Yavuz and Esposito*, 19-47.

CHAPTER SIX

FETHULLAH GÜLEN AND THOMAS MERTON ON SPIRITUALITY AND SOCIAL ACTIVISM

Özgür Koca

Introduction

This study aims to critically compare and contrast the accounts of Fethullah Gülen and Thomas Merton (1915-1968) on the balance of spirituality and action. I argue that there are significant overlaps in their approaches that make it possible to start a scholarly and enriching interaction between the two thinkers. Both Gülen and Merton affirm that "real and solid" spirituality requires a degree of solitude, self-discipline, inward-looking, and renunciation of the worldly pleasures. Yet they also affirm that spirituality is more than an inward search. One's retreat to the center of the soul can and must provide a solid foundation for more effective social activism. To this end, Gülen and Merton present novel approaches to include social activism within the definition of spirituality without rejecting the rich legacy of traditional accounts and practices. The article also points out the differences in their approaches. These points of divergence, however, do not preclude an interaction but rather enrich the dialogue between the two.

In what follows, I will do the following: First, I discuss both Merton's and Gülen's approaches to inward-looking spirituality. Then, I will examine their exegetical strategies to both preserve and transcend traditional accounts of spirituality to make it more relevant to contemporary audiences. Finally, I will delineate the points of convergence and divergence between the two thinkers.

Thomas Merton on the Balance of Contemplation and Action

Thomas Merton was an internationally renowned Catholic monk, writer, poet, and social activist. He authored more than 50 books, and many consider him one of the most influential spiritual writers of the 20th century. After his conversion to Catholicism, he detached himself from the world and spent 27 years as a Trappist monk in the Abbey of Our Lady of Gethsemani. Near the end of his life, Merton transformed from a solitary, contemplative monk into an advocate of nonviolent social activism.

In his early writings, Merton defines spirituality as a journey toward one's spiritual center. His basic diagnosis is that we are detached from God because we are detached from our true selves. To overcome this predicament, one must journey toward the innermost center of the soul where one transcends the illusion of ego and meets God. This requires an inward-looking, solitary search. Solitude, then, is necessary for some "real and solid contemplation." It is in this solitude and quietude that one can gradually distance oneself from the noise of collective life and see the center of the soul more clearly. One thus needs to be isolated from society and discover the "fertile emptiness" in which the true self of the human soul reveals itself, with all its grandeur, like a "paradise tree."[1]

This discernment leads to an awareness of God beyond rational and sensual confines. That is to say, one experiences the presence of God in a way that is not limited by his or her emotional needs, psychological anxieties, and philosophical/theological concepts. Therefore, what really matters in spirituality is an experiential discernment of God, as the term "intuitive contemplation" suggests.

---

[1]   Thomas Merton, *Emblems of a Season of Fury* (New York: New Directions, 1963), 52.

To convey the importance of solitude and quietude for contemplative life, Merton frequently uses the imagery of St. John of the Cross. For
him, St. John of the Cross' metaphor of darkness implies the closure of
the senses to the outer world and, thus, an opening to the inward. The
night of contemplation clouds all distractions and makes the seeker
penetrate all the layers and "deepest intentions"[2] standing before the
virgin point (*le point vierge*) of the soul where we unite with God. In this
contemplative night, the center of the soul where the self and God meet
"shines forth" and becomes discernible. Here, one sees God as the "transcendent source" of our own existence.[3] The illusory self disappears
and is replaced by a new self that is based on God's merciful, continuous sustenance. The discovery of the innermost self and its mysterious
connection to God negates the ego-self. One understands that what is
perceived as real, the ego-self, is actually unreal. This "inner experience," also the title of one of his books, lies at the center of all spirituality and is "the only true joy":

> Our real enemy is within our own castle. It is only because this
> enemy surrounds himself with the images and sensations and
> delights of created things and thus fortifies himself against all
> efforts of grace to dislodge him, that we must necessarily con-
> trol our natural love for good things in order to fight him. . . an
> ego-centered love of the good things of life is a source of dark-
> ness and evil in the world.[4]

Merton sees ascetic self-denial as a form of liberation from ego-
centrism. Asceticism, as Ross Larbrie observes in *The Seven Storey
Mountain*, saves the self from fragmentation.[5] This fragmented self is in
a self-imposed prison and need to be reunited to give itself to God and

---

2   Thomas Merton, *Contemplative Prayer* (New York: Herder and Herder, 1969), 82.
3   Thomas Merton, *The New Man* (New York: Farrar Straus Giroux, 1961), 19.
4   Thomas Merton, *Seasons of Celebration* (New York: Farrar, Straus, Giroux, 1965),
    135.
5   Thomas Merton, *The Seven Storey Mountain* (New York: Harcourt Brace, 1948),
    170.

to others. The act of self-denial is a form of charity. One dies to oneself to resurrect in the "Spirit of the Risen Christ" as a liberated being.[6]

Despite the profundity, power, and beauty of solitary contemplative life, in his later writings and speeches, Merton urges his fellow monks to be aware of the problems of the world and to be part of social change. In such works as *Contemplation in a World of Action*, Merton argues that contemplation could actually be an opportunity for social and political change.[7] A "literalist and antiquarian concept of the contemplative life"[8] should not prevent a monk from being involved in social life. Contemplative life and social activism actually nourish each other.

This new emphasis takes Merton beyond the walls of his monastery. Based on his previous experience with asceticism, he presents a list of arguments for this transformation from almost exclusive accentuation of solitary contemplation to the pursuit of balance between contemplation and action. How?

In *New Seeds of Contemplation*, Merton describes contemplation as the culmination of intellectuality and spirituality.[9] It might manifest itself through creation and daily events or more "religious" moments. The isolated, contemplative periods pave the way for sudden awareness of the presence of the Divine in less isolated moments: in crowds, in moments of haste, or in society. In these moments of awareness, we contact the Divine reality as we do in more solitary circumstances, as if we are "touched by God."[10]

From another perspective, one discovers in contemplation his or her own inner truth through the eyes of God.[11] Contemplation pursues the "inmost ground" of one's life.[12] The discovery of this transcendent

6 Merton, Seasons of Celebration, 143.
7 Thomas Merton, *Contemplation in a World of Action* (New York: Doubleday, 1971).
8 Thomas Merton, *The Hidden Ground of Love: On Religious Experience and Social Concerns* (New York: Farrar Straus Giroux, 1985), 78.
9 Thomas Merton, *New Seeds of Contemplation* (New York: New Directions, 1962), 1.
10 Merton, *New Seeds*, 3.
11 Thomas Merton, *The Inner Experience*, ed. William Shannon (San Francisco: Harper Collins, 2003), 11.
12 Merton, *Contemplative*, 84.

self also allows for the discovery of the transcendent selves of the others who thus deserve respect, justice, and love.

One of the most systematic justifications of Merton's transformation is presented in "Poetry and the Contemplative Life" (1947) and "Poetry and Contemplation: A Reappraisal" (1958).[13] In these works, Merton does not see mutual exclusion between contemplation and action. To present action as a form of contemplation, he presents a threefold approach to contemplation: natural, active, and infused contemplation.

In *natural* contemplation one discerns the traces of the Divine in the forms and processes of nature. Nature is a display of God's beauty. The good in nature reflects God as the Good; the ugly and suffering, in a way, underlies this beauty. God is the mysterious ground of all beings, all Being. The continuous recreation of the world creates a sense of presence before God.

> Beauty of sunlight falling on a tall vase of red and white carnations and green leaves on the altar of the novitiate chapel. The light and dark. The darkness of the fresh, crinkled flower: light, warm and red, all around the darkness. The flower is the same color as blood, but it is in no sense whatever "as red as blood." Not at all! It is as red as a carnation. Only that. This flower, this light, this moment, this silence: Dominus est. Eternity. He passes. He remains. We pass. In and out. He passes. We remain. We are nothing. We are everything. He is in us. He is gone from us. He is not here. We are in Him.[14]

The *infused* contemplation turns toward the inward as opposed to the natural contemplation, which seeks God in the outward. In the hierarchy of contemplations, this represents the culmination, as described

---

13 Thomas Merton, "Poetry and the Contemplative Life," *Figures for an Apocalypse* (New York: New Directions, 1947): 95-111; Thomas Merton, "Poetry and Contemplation: A Reappraisal," *The Literary Essays of Thomas Merton*, ed. Patrick Hart (New York: New Directions, 1981): 338-54.

14 Thomas Merton, *Conjectures of a Guilty Bystander* (New York: Doubleday, 1966), 131.

above. This is Merton's favorite form of contemplation, as the presence of God permeates the soul in the contemplative night.

The *active* contemplation turns toward the social life as opposed to the inward and outward tendencies of infused and natural contemplation. This contemplation is based on the preceding two. One becomes more charitable to "life and to others,"[15] for one sees God's presence not only in his own life but also in the life of the "other," and he or she serves God, human, and God-in-human. What is discovered in the contemplative process remains hidden and dormant until it is manifested in the form of charitable, active contemplation.[16]

As such, for Merton, contemplation is a "solid foundation for every other human striving,"[17] the quintessence of which is to love others "in and for God," realizing the presence of God "in this present life, in the world, and in myself."[18] This form of spirituality necessarily manifests itself in the social dimension.

The revolutionary spirit of the post-war era, human rights activism in the 1960s, popular philosophical currents such as Existentialism and Marxism, and philosophers like Daniel Berrigan, Dorothy Day, and Hannah Arendt also explain Merton's transition from a contemplative life to social activism. For example in "Marxism and Monastic Perspectives," Merton seems to be in agreement with Marx's criticism of capitalist economics and ethics that revolve around self-interest.[19] There are also passages indicating an appreciation of Nietzsche's and Arendt's criticism of asceticism when it leads to suppressing the history-changing individuals and to quietism.

Merton's involvement with existential thought especially in Heidegger's writings, gives him a philosophical reason to value social activism. Heidegger places direct involvement above intellectual and conceptual analysis. What matters is the experience of being, not the

---

15   Merton, *The Inner Experience*, 59.
16   Merton, *The Inner Experience*, 41.
17   Merton, *The Inner Experience*, 152.
18   Merton, *Conjectures*, 320.
19   Thomas Merton, "Marxism and Monastic Perspectives," *The Asian Journal of Thomas Merton* (New York: New Directions, 1973): 334.

conceptualization of being, which is a distortion of its most authentic nature. Merton's asceticism similarly suggests that for a contemplative, there is no *cogito* in the Cartesian sense. Contemplation is not really a function of thought. There is only SUM, I AM in contemplation.[20] If so, then experiential participation in being is more convenient than the distanced rational conceptualization of being. This, I believe, is another cause of Merton's development of a practical form of asceticism.

The idea of integrating asceticism and deep concern for social affairs seems to contradict the early Christian monks' emphasis on disciplining the flesh through strict monastic exercises, such as celibacy. However, in the sixth century, St. Benedict, the father of modern monasticism, moderated the ascetic excesses and reformulated monasticism for "ordinary men." Merton holds that this Benedictine form of asceticism is more appropriate for modern times. He writes:

> St. Benedict shifted the whole impact of asceticism to the interior — from the flesh to the will ... Extraordinary mortifications were forbidden or discouraged. The sacrifices that really mattered to him were those that were exacted in secrecy from the deepest veins of selfhood.[21]

In short, penitential acts do not actually bring balance to spiritual life, but rather infuse spirit with a sense of "revenge." A bad temper would be the fruit of this form of asceticism. Thus, instead of trying to annihilate body for the sake of spirit, the two should unite. He also argues that the Bible does not advocate for the idea of complete severance of the soul from the body. This idea was constructed in a specific context due to the influence of other forms of asceticism, such as Neo-Platonism and the oppression of political power. The exclusive concentration on contemplation is contrary to the Christian ideal. Contemplation and action support each other in a Christian life, as exemplified by St. Benedict.[22]

---

20 Merton, *New Seeds*, 9.
21 Ross Labrie, "Asceticism in the Writings of Thomas Merton," *Logos* 13 (Winter 2010): 160-181.
22 Merton, *Contemplative*, 143-44.

Finally, Merton views contemplation as an opportunity for better social activism. Contemplation enlarges one's perspective. The temporary solitude of the monk situates him beyond the tumults of social life, therefore allowing him to have a view from the outside. A monk's lifestyle, consisting of physical poverty and abandonment of fame and ego, makes him a stronger participant in social activism since he does not have much to lose and can risk more. Likewise, social activism fails when it is merely a guise for self-affirmation.[23]

Fethullah Gülen on Spirituality and Service

Sufism plays a significant role in Gülen's thought and practice. Sufism denotes a spectrum of ideas and behaviors that are highly diversified yet revolve around certain common tenets. Sufi orders are differentiated from each other by their specific emphases and practices. For some, it means practicing religion with spiritual depth. For others, it is primarily an attempt to attain a higher knowledge of the Divine (*ma'rifah*). For others, it is essentially a way to develop a relationship with God based on love (*muhabba*). This difference, however, is one of accentuation, as a Sufi order emphasizing *ma'rifah* will also have an element of *muhabba* and vice versa.

Where do we locate Gülen in this context of highly differentiated yet deeply intertwined appearances of Islamic spirituality? Thomas Michel cites an interesting passage from Gülen in which he combines differing definitions of Sufism to capture its fluidity. He writes, for example:

> The Islamic spiritual life based on asceticism, regular worship, abstention from all major and minor sins, sincerity and purity of intention, love and yearning, and the individual's admission of his essential impotence and destitution became the subject-matter of Sufism.[24]

---

[23] Merton, "Poetry and Contemplation: A Reappraisal," 339.

[24] Fethullah Gülen, "What is Sufism?" in *Fountain Magazine* 47 (July-September 2004): 49.

These definitions explicate what is important for Gülen in Sufism: It is to strike a balance between exoteric (*zahir*) and esoteric (*batin*) dimensions of Islam. He, therefore, diverges from those who seem to perceive religious rituals as unnecessary after the attainment of a certain spiritual level. For Gülen, no matter what one's spiritual elevation is, one must not abandon the law, *Shari'a*. Religion should not also be reduced to following certain rituals. Spirituality is like the sap of religion, nurturing it from within. Sufism and *Shari'a* are complementary. They resemble, to use Rumi's analogy, a fruit with its kernel and shell, which both need each other and the unity of which makes the totality of the fruit. A kernel without a shell is unprotected and could reduce spirituality into disguised egoism and hedonism. A shell without a kernel is just a dry husk. As such, Gülen's perception is fully in accordance with his tutor, Said Nursi, and with larger schools of Sufism, such as Qadiriyya and Naqshbandiyya.[25]

For Gülen, Sufism is a journey towards God who is absolutely one and simultaneously transcendent and immanent. Humans are created and equipped to take this journey.[26] This journey ends with a deeper realization of God's presence (*ihsan*) and the absolute dependence of our existences to God at each moment (*yaqin*). It also leads to the purification of the heart and the practice of religion without searching for disguised egoistic pleasures under the garment of religiosity (*ikhlas*). It is to live one's life as if one is in the presence of God at all times with awe and joy (*taqwa*):

> Knowledge of God does not consist of abstract knowledge; in its true form, it is transformed into love. We cannot remain indifferent to someone in whom we believed and then grew to know well. After belief and knowledge comes love. Love is the crown of belief in God and knowledge of Him ... sacred knowledge increases, giving rise to increasing in love, which causes knowledge to increase still further.[27]

---

25 Fethullah Gülen, *The Emerald Hills of the Heart: Key Concepts in the Practice of Sufism* (New Jersey: The Light, 2004): 9.

26 Gülen, *The Emerald Hills*, 118.

27 Cited in Heon C. Kim, "Sufism and Dialogue in the Hizmet Movement," *Hizmet Studies Review* 2, no. 2 (Spring 2015): 33-49.

Gülen, in this passage, links the concepts of knowledge and love to each other. The more one knows God, the more one loves God. According to Sufi cosmology, the world is a multiplicity of the mirrors on which God's names and attributes are continuously displayed. The cosmos is a collectivity of signs (*ayat*), and Islamic spirituality encourages humans to focus on these signs, as they are themselves a microcosm of and able to decipher these signs. Sufism, by contemplating on the inward and the outward, leads to further discovery and thus knowledge of the Divine. This, however, is not an "abstract" and disinterested knowledge, but rather, it leads to a greater love.

In a similar vein to Thomas Merton, Gülen is not in favor of reducing Islamic spiritual experience to the relationships between God and individual humans. Spirituality cannot be confined to exclusive, individual inwardness. The implications of spirituality for social life must be traced. How?

First, Gülen writes that the concept of love, which is so central to Islamic spirituality, necessarily manifests itself in a social dimension. "Overflowing with Divine Love" enables one to realize that "the universe is a cradle of brotherhood." It also entails "giving preference or precedence to the well-being and happiness of others."[28]

Secondly, "asceticism" is a nuanced term for Gülen. Sufism enables individuals to deepen their awareness of themselves as devotees of God. While a certain kind of renunciation of the transient, material world is envisioned here, it does not and must not lead to total rejection of the world. The asceticism of Sufism awakens the contemplative ascetic "to the reality of the other world, which is turned toward God's Beautiful Names." The world has, then, several faces. What is eschewed is not the face that reflects the Divine qualities, but the one that "veils" it. In accordance with this idea, Gülen advises a rejection of the world in the heart but not in action (*kesben degil kalben terketme*). Therefore he sees escapist mysticism as rejected.[29]

---

28 Kim, "Sufism and Dialogue," 33-49.
29 Gülen, *The Emerald Hills*, 72-73.

Thirdly, Sufism employs a specific vocabulary to express the experiences of Sufis in their journey towards God. These are called stations (*maqamat*) and states (*ahwal*). Gülen inherits this vocabulary, the roots of which can be traced back to Qur'an and Sunna enriched thanks to the rich interpretive efforts of Sufis and other exegetes over the centuries. In the *Emerald Hills of the Heart*, Gülen introduces his readers to terms such as repentance (*tawba*), sincerity (*ikhlas*), contentment (*ridha*), contemplation (*tafakkur*), and remembrance (*dhikr*). His exegetical strategy, as noted by Enes Ergene and Dogu Ergil, is that he preserves the specific traditional meanings of these concepts, but he also frequently offers fresh approaches to these concepts to emphasize their implications for social life. As it were, he reinterprets these concepts without losing their traditional meanings.

Contemplation, for example, is traditionally understood, almost exclusively, as "reading," "witnessing," and understanding the Divine Names and Attributes manifested in the world and as pondering upon the mysteries of the God-cosmos relationship, and as delving into the depths of one's heart. As such, traditional Islamic denotation of contemplation comes close to what Thomas Merton calls infused and natural contemplation. In a similar vein, Gülen values the traditional meanings of contemplation, while aiming to extend the implications of this deeply inward-looking search to the social domain. Thus for Gülen, contemplation also means to ponder upon society, its problems, and the remedies to these problems. This is "giving contemplation its proper object."[30]

Privacy (*halwat*) and seclusion ('*uzlat*) within the context of Sufism is usually understood as an "initiate's going into retreat to dedicate all of his or her time to worshipping God under the guidance and supervision of a spiritual master."[31] Gülen accepts that temporary seclusion can have great benefits for the human soul. The most authentic forms of seclusion and privacy can be found in the lives of great exemplars,

---

[30] Fethullah Gülen, *So That Others May Live: A Fethullah Gülen Reader*, ed. Erkan Kurt (Bludome Press, 2013), 46.
[31] Gülen, *The Emerald Hills*, 141.

such as Moses, Jesus, and Muhammad. In some cases, this form of retreat is necessary for deeper concentration. Gülen again preserves and values all the traditional meanings attributed to the terms "privacy and seclusion." However, he also suggests that "since the purpose of seclusion is to purify the heart of the love which is not directed toward God and to be always with the beloved, those who always feel the presence of God while living among people and who continuously discern the Divine Unity amidst multiplicity are regarded as always being with God in seclusion. Similar to Merton, Gülen urges people to be careful against the more insidious dangers of seclusion. One can spend his life in seclusion but still fail to "purify his heart" from attachment to ego. Thus, for him, the most perfect form of seclusion is "in the world but not of the world." To use his analogy, one should be like a pair of compasses with "one arm in the midst of people and one in realm of the Divine."[32]

Piety or reverential awe (*taqwa*) is usually defined in the context of Islamic spirituality as "protecting oneself from God's punishment by performing His commands and observing His prohibitions." For Gülen, in its more comprehensive meaning, *taqwa* denotes following God's commands not only as they are expressed in the Qur'anic revelation, but also in the book of the universe.[33] The message of the universe is also a continuous Divine revelation. *Taqwa* entails a conscious relationship with the Divine text and context.[34] Again, Gülen offers a more comprehensive meaning than traditionally attributed to the term "*taqwa*" that can include a more active way of being in the natural and social world. Similarly, "being content with little" or a "pious lifestyle" actually prepares one to involve him or herself more efficiently in social life.[35]

Gülen emphasizes being where the inward and outward meet, as evinced in his definition of metaphysics: "Metaphysics is to comprehend existence as a unity of its observable and unobservable aspects"

---

[32] Gülen, *The Emerald Hills*, 141.
[33] Gülen, *The Emerald Hills*, 81.
[34] Gülen, *The Emerald Hills*, 76.
[35] Ergil, 50.

and the "ability of love to perceive reality as a whole."[36] This emphasis is observable in the activities of the Hizmet movement, which he inspired. The participants of this movement have presented highly successful examples of social involvement. They have established, for example, schools, universities, interfaith/intrafaith dialogue institutes, media organizations, newspapers, humanitarian aid organizations, and healthcare institutes. In these activities, the vertical relationship with the Creator strengthens the horizontal relationship with the created. Thus, there is no dichotomy between the inward and outward journey. The culmination of human perfection is sought in this balance.

A Common Search for Equilibrium

Merton and Gülen promote a common search for a spirituality that is, on the one hand, deeply inward-looking, yet on the other hand extends to the natural and social domains. Spirituality is not an escapist behavior but rather a temporary retreat to the center of the soul, only to come back with a refreshed and enlarged perspective and revitalized ambition to contribute the world.

For both thinkers, spirituality is a journey to the center of one's being: for Merton, *le point vierge* and, for Gülen, the heart (*qalb*). Merton recommends going to the virgin point of the soul to transcend the ego and attain communion with God. This communion, in Merton's work, remains ineffable. Similarly, Gülen sees the heart as the most comprehensive mirror for the manifestations of the Divine secrets: The heart is "the polished mirror in which Divine knowledge is reflected."[37] God is known experientially through the heart, and though philosophical and theological conceptualizations are necessary to a certain extent, they are not sufficient to convey the nature of this meeting with God in the heart.

Both Merton and Gülen seem to value temporary retreat from the world. Isolation from social life is not an end in itself but rather a means to an end. Merton maintains that solitude is necessary for "real and

---

[36] Gülen, *So That Others*, 45.
[37] Gülen, *The Emerald Hills*, 24.

solid contemplation." Despite his praise of social life, as a monk, he never loses the desire for solitary contemplation. The monastery remains "a barrier and a defence against the world."[38] Gülen appreciates the indispensability of temporary seclusion as exemplified in the lives of the Prophets and Sufi masters. It is only natural to detach oneself from the noise of the world to focus on the soul.

Merton and Gülen also agree that spirituality brings great joy. For Merton, "true joy" lies at the center of spirituality. Gülen agrees with this belief: Knowledge and love of God lead to a great spiritual joy (lezzet-i ruhani).

The term "asceticism" for both thinkers is a nuanced term. Merton favors St. Benedict's moderate approach to asceticism, which shifted the whole impact "from the flesh to the interior" as opposed to the earlier forms of Christian asceticism, which leaned toward strict mortifications. This ascetic separation of the soul and body is a preparatory step; ascetic detachment is not an end in itself, but rather, it should open itself to "charity, mercy." Asceticism should not be based on the idea of intrinsic negativity of the world and the body, and it should not lead to an estrangement from the well-being of others. Merton believes humans need to go back to the "way we are." Gülen similarly criticizes the excesses of asceticism and instead suggests the renunciation of the world in the heart, not in action. The world is not intrinsically diabolic, so it must be loved and cultivated. Moreover, this involvement in the world allows one to see the reality of the world as a mirror of God's Beautiful Names (asma al-husna).

Another point of convergence is that both Merton and Gülen see spirituality as a form of liberation from egoism. Merton's act of self-denial and Gülen's act of dying to himself (nafy) lead to a new form of life in which one goes beyond the egotistic confines. "Self-emptying" and "self-forgetfulness" also prepare one to serve individuals in need.

The two thinkers employ similar exegetical strategies to achieve an equilibrium of spirituality and social activism. Both urge their audiences to be aware of social problems and to be part of the solutions

---

[38] Merton, The Seven Storey, 32.

through activism. Merton and Gülen hold that one's inward journey is an indispensable part of one's outward journey, for they nourish each other. Namely, in spirituality, one discovers the potential of human spirit and witnesses the same potential in others. The presence of God in the soul and in the world sacralizes the world. For both thinkers, the sacralization of the other and the world leads to interactions based on respect and love. Herein, as Merton puts it, spirituality becomes a "solid foundation" for social activism. As Merton takes spirituality beyond the walls of his monastery, Gülen takes it beyond Sufi orders.

Both thinkers also have a nuanced approach to contemplation. For Merton, as mentioned above, there are three types of contemplation: infused, natural, and active. Infused contemplation focuses on *le point vierge*, natural contemplation discerns the traces of God in natural processes, and active contemplation ponders upon social problems. Similarly for Gülen, the term contemplation (*tafakkur*) means different things in different contexts. Sometimes, contemplation witnesses to the reflections of the Divine Names on the loci of the created order (*afaki tafakkur*), sometimes it means an inward search (*enfusi tafakkur*), and sometimes it is to think about social problems and their solutions.

Merton and Gülen want to resuscitate somewhat marginalized traditions in their own religious contexts. Merton is drawn to medieval Christian mysticism, which is more clearly observable through his emphasis on "intuitive contemplation." Gülen, in his Emerald Hills of the Heart, aims to bring Sufi terminology back to life with modifications. Merton and Gülen value the appreciation of traditional spiritual teachings and practices.

Despite these overlaps, there also seem to be several points of divergence. First, Gülen does not engage with the dominant philosophical currents of the 20th century, as Merton does with Marxism and Existentialism. Merton intellectually interacts with these ideologies and occasionally modifies his convictions in light of them. Gülen, however, almost exclusively draws on the rich Islamic spiritual tradition.

Secondly, Merton, based on his travels in Asia and studies on Eastern religions, especially Buddhism, develops a more eclectic spiritual style. He frequently draws on Buddhist monastic life, practices, and

Taoist doctrines. Gülen appears not to use other religions as points of reference to make his cases. Gülen seems to be much more traditional than Merton in this regard.

Another difference between Merton and Gülen is their perceptions of the God-cosmos relationship. Merton constructs this relationship in a non-dualistic way. For example, he writes, "Zen is the ontological *awareness of pure being beyond subject and object.*"[39] Merton also attempts to reconcile Zen and Daoist non-dualism with Christian mysticism. This is only natural for Merton, as his spiritual style accentuates meeting God in the virgin point of the soul. This requires that the separation between the self and God is not ultimate; there is a continuation. Gülen, however, seems to lean toward dualism, because non-dualism appears to collapse the distinction between God and humans. Gülen urges his readers to stay in the domain of discernment (*farq*) between the Absolute (*mutlaq*) and the relative or contingent (*izafi*). This discernment is followed by a desire to move toward the Absolute being, for the contingent cannot remain aloof of the Absolute. Though Merton accentuates a non-dualistic spirituality and Gülen tends toward dualism, here the difference seems to be one of accentuation, not of privation.

To conclude, there are significant commonalities between Merton and Gülen. These two influential thinkers and activists advocate for a socially active form of spirituality. Merton predominantly draws from Christian mysticism, while Gülen turns to the rich legacy of Sufism. Although they depart from different places, their perspectives frequently meet. They present the implications of traditional spiritual teachings and practices for contemporary audience. They maintain that social activism is inherent in these teachings, provided that they are properly and comprehensively understood. To this end, Merton and Gülen offer novel interpretations while preserving the traditional content. This allows them to be traditional and contemporary at once, and it explains their success in making spirituality relevant in contemporary times.

---

[39] Thomas Merton, *Mystics and Zen Masters* (New York: Farrar, Straus and Giroux, 1969), 14.

References

Ergene, Enes. Gelenegin Modern Caga Tanikligi, Yeni Akademi Yayinlari, 2005.

Ergil, Doğu. *Fethullah Gülen and The Gülen Movement in 100 Questions.* New York: Blue Dome Press, 2012.

Gülen, Fethullah. *So That Others May Live: A Fethullah Gülen Reader.* Edited by Erkan Kurt.Bludome Press, 2013.

———. *The Emerald Hills of the Heart: Key Concepts in the Practice of Sufism.* New Jersey: The Light, 2004.

———. "What is Sufism?" In *Fountain Magazine* 47 (July-September 2004): 47-50.

Kim, Heon C. "Sufism and Dialogue in the Hizmet Movement." *Hizmet Studies Review* 2, no. 2 (Spring 2015): 33-49.

Labrie, Ross. "Asceticism in the Writings of Thomas Merton." *Logos* 13 (Winter 2010): 160-81

Merton, Thomas. *Conjectures of a Guilty Bystander.* New York: Doubleday, 1966.

———. *Contemplation in a World of Action.* New York: Doubleday, 1971.

———. *Contemplative Prayer.* New York: Herder and Herder, 1969.

———. *The Courage for Truth: The Letters of Thomas Merton to Writers.* Edited by Christine Bochen. New York: Farrar Straus Giroux, 1993.

———. *Emblems of a Season of Fury.* New York: New Directions, 1963.

———. *The Hidden Ground of Love: On Religious Experience and Social Concerns.* New York: Farrar Straus Giroux, 1985.

———. *The Inner Experience.* Edited by William Shannon. San Francisco: Harper Collins, 2003.

———. "Marxism and Monastic Perspectives." *The Asian Journal of Thomas Merton* (New York: New Directions, 1973): 326-43.

———. *Mystics and Zen Masters.* New York: Farrar, Straus and Giroux, 1969.

———. *The New Man.* New York: Farrar Straus Giroux, 1961.

———. *New Seeds of Contemplation.* New York: New Directions, 1962.

———. "Poetry and the Contemplative Life." *Figures for an Apocalypse.* (New York: New Directions, 1947): 95-111.

———. "Poetry and Contemplation: A Reappraisal." *The Literary Essays of Thomas Merton.* Edited by Patrick Hart. (New York: New Directions, 1981): 338-54.

———. *The Seven Storey Mountain.* New York: Harcourt Brace, 1948.

———. *Seasons of Celebration.* New York: Farrar, Straus, Giroux, 1965. Michel, Thomas. http://hizmetmovement.blogspot.com/2012/07/Gülen-move-ment-sufi-type-spirituality.html

PART TWO

GÜLEN AMONG HISTORICAL PEERS

CHAPTER SEVEN

DESIDERIUS ERASMUS AND FETHULLAH GÜLEN: INTERCULTURAL AND INTERFAITH BRIDGE-BUILDERS

Pim Valkenberg

I n this essay, I will consider the nature and role of intercultural and interfaith bridge-building and compare, in this regard, Fethullah Gülen with the famous Dutch philosopher and theologian Desiderius Erasmus (1466/9-1536). I will sketch some of the similarities between Gülen and Erasmus in their efforts to promote peace-building and communication, but I will also pay attention to a major difference: While Erasmus explicitly refers to his missionary intention to proclaim the Christian faith, Gülen refers to his Muslim background in a different way. Considering this difference, I will conclude by asking whether the implicit character of the reference to religious inspiration in the movement that is inspired by Fethullah Gülen might be one of the reasons explaining the suspicion that has recently been raised against this movement in Germany and the Netherlands.

Intercultural and Interfaith Bridge-Builders

In the fall of 2008, Loyola University Maryland chose Eboo Patel's book *Acts of Faith* (Boston 2007) as a common text for all incoming new students. All freshmen were supposed to read the book during the summer so they could participate in various discussions about it throughout their first year. They also had the opportunity to discuss the book with Patel himself when he came to campus that fall, and to respond to his invitation to become interfaith bridge builders themselves.

One of the good things about Eboo Patel's book is that it is not difficult for young adults — especially those studying at a Jesuit institution — to identify with Patel in the sense that he had been involved in much service work as a young student in Chicago, while being unaware of the religious backgrounds of the institutions where he performed this work. More specifically, Patel talks about his engagement in Dorothy Day's Catholic Workers movement, but he does not seem to recognize how his own search for religious community life echoes the religious quest of Dorothy Day and her "Long Loneliness."[1] Only later, in an interview with the Dalai Lama, Patel starts to realize that as an American Muslim from India, he has a religious background of his own, and that it has shaped his life all along. This experience incites him to engage in interfaith youth work with the strong conviction that his mission is not to weaken the religious identity of the youth, but to "strengthen their religious identities by creating a safe space where they could talk about their faith."[2] Precisely because he was able to recognize how his own faith shaped his acts, Patel was able to build the Interfaith Youth Core in Chicago, an organization that now extends nationally and globally, and that offers many initiatives to combine interfaith education and service-learning.[3] Among others, his organization started Bridge-Builders, an internet community of future leaders for interfaith youth work.[4]

Toward the end of his book, Patel mentions the names of the bridge-builders that inspired him in his religious quest: Nelson Mandela, Martin

---

[1] Dorothy Day, *The Long Loneliness: The Autobiography Of The Legendary Catholic Social Activist* (New York: Harpercollins, 1997).

[2] Eboo Patel, *Acts of Faith: The Story of an American Muslim, the Struggle for the Soul of a Generation*, (Boston: Beacon Press, 2007), 166.

[3] Eboo Patel & Patrice Brodeur, *Building the Interfaith Youth Movement: Beyond Dialogue to Action*, (Lanham Md: Rowman & Littlefield, 2006, Eds).

[4] See bridge-builders.ning.com

Luther King, Mahatma Gandhi, and Dorothy Day. We tend to think of them as old, wise men and women, but they started young and were inspired by their faith, so Patel thinks they might be suitable models for contemporary students who often are willing to work for peace and justice, but have trouble articulating the faith background that inspires them in their acts of faith. This forms an interesting backdrop for my consideration of the interfaith bridge-building of Erasmus and Gülen.

Erasmus and Gülen as Promoters of Peace and Education

In the Netherlands, the Cosmicus Foundation organized a number of symposia at several universities in 2004 and 2005, in which scholars discussed the contributions of several "forerunners in peace" in hopes of inspiring students to also engage in building peace through education and interfaith dialogue. In these symposia, several speakers focused on Desiderius Erasmus and Fethullah Gülen, together with Pope John Paul II, Mother Theresa, the Dalai Lama, Saint Francis of Assisi, Mevlana Jalaluddin Rumi, and Rabbi Nachman of Breslov.[5] Several years later, something similar happened in Rotterdam, the Netherlands, where the local Dialogue Academy organized a small conference on Gülen and Erasmus on the occasion of the birthday of Erasmus of Rotterdam. Maybe the most significant feature of this conference was that it took place three months after Fethullah Gülen and his movement were accused in a well-known Dutch television show of Islamizing tendencies that would lead to Muslim isolationism and indoctrination. Questions were raised in Parliament, and several political parties asked that the government withdraw its subsidies to Gülen-oriented organizations. As a consequence, the Dutch organization *Humanistisch Verbond*, which sees itself as the heir of Erasmus' humanism and the defender of non-religious worldviews, withdrew its contribution to this conference on Gülen and Erasmus. Fortunately, the humanistic Rotterdam Erasmus House Foundation kept its promise to be a co-host and organizer, so Muslims, Christians, and Humanists together were able to

---

5   Gurkan Celik, *et al., Voorlopers In De Vrede*, (Budel: Damon, 2005).

share their opinions on Gülen and Erasmus as sources of inspiration for peace and dialogue.

One of the reasons for my reference to this conference in Rotterdam is that most people in Europe would think of Erasmus as one of the first great humanists, rather than as an engaged theologian and Christian. Yet for Erasmus, the two things go together: For example, in his major scholarly work, a critical edition of the New Testament, the desire to reconstruct the authentic text of the New Testament is paired with a desire to return to the peaceful and simple faith of Jesus and his followers. Therefore, if we associate Desiderius Erasmus with humanism, or even with the Greco-Roman foundations of present-day Europe, we should be aware that the humanism of his time was different from the humanism professed today. Because of this, the digital biography of Erasmus on the website of the *Erasmus Center for Early Modern Studies* — a joint initiative of the Erasmus University Rotterdam and the Rotterdam City Library — comes to the conclusion that "Erasmus is more of a Christian than everybody seems to think nowadays."[6] We will notice how this makes Erasmus different from Gülen in a moment; but first, we may observe how the two great thinkers are similar in their concern for education and peace-building.

Muhammad Fethullah Gülen was born in 1941 in Erzurum in the North-Eastern part of Anatolia. He was educated as a scholar of Islam in the tradition of Said Nursi, an important Qur'anic scholar in the waning age of the Ottoman Empire who distanced himself from Kemal Atatürk's secular Turkey. Nursi built a community of students of the Qur'an, mediated by his own series of spiritual and scientific meditations on the Qur'an, *Risale'i Nur*. Although Fethullah Gülen was never a student in the Nursi movement, the way in which Nursi's students lived and learned together in *dershanes* may be seen as a model for Gülen's educational initiatives.[7] The second major influence on Gülen during

6   See www.erasmus.org
7   Bekim Agai, *Zwischen Netzwerk Und Diskurs: Das Bildungsnetzwerk Um Fethullah Gülen (Geb. 1938): Die Flexible Umsetzung Modernen Islamischen Gedankenguts* (Schenefeld: EbVerlag, 2004). Celik, Gurkan & Pim Valkenberg, "Gülen's Approach to Dialogue and Peace: Its Theoretical Background and Some Practical Perspectives," *The International Journal of Diversity in Organisations, Communities & Nations* 7, no. 1 (2007): 29-37.

his youth was the Sufi path in the tradition of Jalaluddin Rumi and Yunus Emre. Between 1966 and 1981, Gülen functioned as imam and teacher in several mosques and schools, and spread his ideas among a growing number of students. He tried to form a new "golden generation" of faithful Muslims who would be able to rekindle the fire of true Islam. These ideals might be similar to the ideals of those who we are now used to addressing as fundamentalists, but Gülen combines theological conservatism with an amazing openness to the modern Western world. In many of his speeches and columns, he does not only refer to the classical sources of Islam, but to Western philosophers, scientists, and political thinkers as well. Dialogue, peace, and tolerance between religions, cultures, and civilizations are his consistent trademarks.[8] Consequently, every short biography mentions Gülen's encounters with national and international religious leaders, culminating in an encounter with Pope John Paul II in 1998. This encounter marked the end of the second period in Gülen's life in which he developed into a national religious symbol in Turkey and in which his followers founded a number of journals, TV-stations, schools, and scientific organizations. Around the turn of the century, Gülen withdrew from the Turkish political scene to lead a secluded life in the U.S. for political and health reasons. While his personal voice is seldom heard, his followers are rapidly extending their influence in many countries in the world, partly through various educational institutions, and partly through dialogue foundations and welfare organizations.

In a certain sense, Fethullah Gülen speaks more through his organizations than through his words. He has written a number of books, but they all consist of short essays, much in the style of a weekly newspaper column. Many of the issues that he discusses are germane to the Muslim tradition, such as the importance of Prophet Muhammad or the central states and stages in the Sufi path, but he alternates these with issues of general importance such as compassion, free will, killing an innocent, and respect for humankind, to mention just a few of the

8   Ali Ünal & Alphonse Williams, *Advocate of Dialogue: Fethullah Gülen* (Fairfax: The Fountain, 2000, Comp).

recent titles on Gülen's website in English.[9] It is precisely this combination of traditional Islamic wisdom and openness for central Western values that makes Gülen a bridge-builder. Without this Islamic background, Gülen's thoughts would have been superficial; without his openness to the Western world of thinking, he would not be able to speak to a new generation of Muslims living in the West.

Fethullah Gülen is probably most well-known globally because of the hundreds of educational institutions that have been founded by persons who belong to Gülen's educational network.[10] While these private schools clearly aim at the highest standards of education according to the laws of education in the countries of their residence, they are non-denominational in the sense that Islam is not taught in these schools and that the students and teachers are religiously diverse. In fact, in many instances the majority of the students are non-Muslims. When we compare these educational initiatives in the name of Gülen with educational initiatives in the name of Erasmus, we see that Erasmus is most often associated with scholarly activities rather than with education in general: from the Erasmus University in Rotterdam to the European Union's Erasmus Programme for Student Mobility. Most of these initiatives focus on the idea of promoting the humanities as the core of advanced education. In both cases, the central focus is on the ideals of academic excellence and of building a generation of future students that will be better equipped to face the problems of the future.

Erasmus was well aware that warfare – especially religious warfare – was one of the biggest challenges for his educational ideals, so he frequently lamented the political and ecclesial situation in the 16th century that was so full of conflicts.[11] One of his meditations on war was in

---

[9] See en.fgulen.com
[10] Agai, *Zwischen Netzwerk Und Diskurs*; Ian Williams, "The Vision of Education within Pluralistic Societies in the Thought of Fethullah Gülen: The Contribution of Non-Denominational Education Towards Inter-Religious and Communal Understanding, Peace and Identity," *Peaceful Coexistence. Fethullah Gülen's Initiatives In The Contemporary World*, (London: Leeds Metropolitan University Press, 2007): 407-415.
[11] Patty Bange, "*Dulce Bellum Inexpertis:* Desiderius Erasmus Over Oorlog En Vrede," *Voorlopers In De Vrede* (Budel: Damon, 2005): 17-30.

fact a commentary on the famous adage *Dulce bellum inexpertis*, "Sweet is war for those who have never experienced it." A few years later, Erasmus wrote another meditation in the form of a lament by Lady Peace.[12] Just like Nicholas of Cusa two generations before him, he dreamt of a situation in which the religions could unite and a *Peace of Faith* could become possible. Small wonder that Erasmus was deeply bothered by the threatening schism in the Western Church between Catholics and Lutherans, and that he tried everything to promote peace and harmony between the two parties, which in the end estranged him from both. Erasmus insisted that peace between religious people should be the rule; that is the example that Christ gave us. In the end, however, the historical situation proved stronger than Erasmus' ideals.

Again, there might be a parallel here with Fethullah Gülen, who promotes love, tolerance, and dialogue as the highest values of humankind.[13] In his writings, Gülen often states that dialogue should not be a possibility, but the religious duty of every Muslim. He quotes a *hadith* (traditional saying) by the Prophet as follows: "true Muslims are those who harm no one with their words and actions and who are the most trustworthy representatives of universal peace."[14] Gülen reminds us that the very word "*muslim*" is derived from a verb with one meaning of "to feel safe" with someone, or "to be at peace" with someone.

Gülen takes this interpretation of what it means to be a Muslim as his hermeneutical rule for reading the Qur'an: The normal situation of relations between Muslims and others should be a situation of peace; if the Qur'an seems to call for war, then there should be a specific reason for it. Gülen explains that the Qur'an may warn Muslims against specific Jews or Christians, but that Muslims should generally strive to live peacefully with Jews, Christians, and others. "Peaceful settlement is always better," he says, explaining Qur'an 4:128.[15] It is in line with this

---

[12] In Latin: *Querela Pacis*
[13] Fethullah Gülen, *Love and the Essence of Being Human*, (Istanbul: Journalists and Writers Foundation, 2004).
[14] Ünal and Williams, *Advocate of Dialogue*, 248
[15] Gülen, *Love and the Essence of Being Human*, 167

reasoning that Gülen often argues that we should forget about the hateful relations of the past, but concentrate on what we have in common.

Again, Erasmus and Gülen seem to converge here in their stress on education, religion, and dialogue as means toward peace, but there is a difference as well, and that will be the subject of the next section of this essay.

Erasmus and Gülen: The Role of Their Religious Backgrounds

There is one piece of Erasmus' writing that seems to create a problem for our topic: In reply to the siege of Vienna by the Ottomans in 1529, Erasmus wrote a little treatise on the usefulness of a war with the Turks. Apparently, his vision of religion as a peaceful power did not extend to Muslims. On the one hand, he suggests that the invasion of the Turks in the heart of Europe is God's penalty for the deep divide within Christianity. On the other hand, Erasmus seems to suggest that we can overcome this disunity by making a common front against the Turks. While dismissing the idea of a physical war against the Turks, Erasmus suggests that we should wage war against our own souls that often diverge from the true religion — an interesting parallel with the idea of a greater *jihad* against one's soul in mystical Islam — and that we should try to solve the Turkish intrusion by sending them missionaries who will proclaim the true Christian faith.[16] So it seems that the Christian humanism of Erasmus extends to tolerance between Catholics and Protestants, but not to tolerance between Christians and Muslims.

At this point, Fethullah Gülen seems to be a better bridge-builder between the Abrahamic religions, since his plea for tolerance and dialogue explicitly includes Jews and Christians.[17] Let me summarize his view in a characteristic quotation and add a few comments: "Interfaith dialog is a must today, and the first step in establishing it is forgetting

---

[16] Bange, *Dulce Bellum Inexpertis*, 27

[17] Fethullah Gülen, *The Necessity of Interfaith Dialog: A Muslim Perspective* (Somerset N.J.: The Light, 2004); Celik and Valkenberg, "Gülen's Approach to Dialogue and Peace"

the past, ignoring polemical arguments, and giving precedence to common points, which far outnumber polemical ones."[18] Of course I can understand why Gülen urges us to forget the often-troublesome history of polemics and to come to a more positive approach;[19] generally speaking, a meaningful dialogue can only be sought when we start with the common points and not with the contested issues. Moreover, almost every Muslim who is willing to engage in dialogue hastens to underscore the positive side of a religion that is so often associated with violence and terrorism in the popular press. Yet I am not so sure whether it is a wise idea to forget about the past, especially since I am inclined to think that we might learn more from our differences than from our commonalities.[20] However, I must admit that Gülen is in good company: No less authority than the Second Vatican Council pleads, after reminding us about the many historical quarrels and dissensions between Christians and Muslims, "to forget the past, and urges that a sincere effort be made to achieve mutual understanding."[21]

Yet my fear is that Gülen's biggest asset as an interfaith bridge-builder may at some point become a drawback as well. In most of Gülen's publications that have been translated into English, he seems to advocate a dialogue between religions and cultures in very general terms; concepts such as love, tolerance, dialogue, humanity, hope, and activism are clearly chosen to facilitate a common ground for dialogue.[22] But to outsiders these concepts are barely recognizable as having the meaning that Gülen assigns to them. There can be no doubt that Gülen

---

[18] Gülen, *The Necessity of Interfaith Dialog*, 7

[19] Norman Daniel, *Islam and the West: The Making of an Image* (Oxford: Oneworld, 1993); Hugh Goddard, *Christians & Muslims: From Double Standards to Mutual Understanding* (London And New York: Routledge Curzon, 1995).

[20] Jonathan Sacks, *The Dignity of Difference: How to Avoid the Clash of Civilizations* (London And New York: Continuum, 2002); Pim Valkenberg, *Sharing Lights on the Way to God: Muslim-Christian Dialogue and Theology in the Context of Abrahamic Partnership* (Amsterdam – New York: Rodopi, 2006): xii

[21] *Nostra Aetate* 3; Francesco Gioia, *Interreligious Dialogue: The Official Teaching of the Catholic Church from the Second Vatican Council to John Paul Ii (1963-2005)* (Boston: Pauline, 2006 Ed.)

[22] Gülen, *Love and the Essence of Being Human*

argues as a Muslim scholar, and therefore these terms for him have specific meanings that are connected to key texts and interpretations in the Islamic tradition; but this specific Islamic "coloring" barely shines through in the texts that are published by his supporters for a broader public, so they could easily be read as just general appeals to love, tolerance, dialogue, and humanity. For most Muslims, it will be clear how Gülen's primary motivation for dialogue is grounded in the tradition of Islam, but outsiders are not likely to get access to this motivation.

The perceived distance between Gülen's personal adherence to the Islamic tradition and the more general character of some of his writings is reflected in the distance between the personal piety of many supporters of organizations founded by Mr. Gülen and the absence of references to this faith background in public statements byTurkish Muslims in the Netherlands who are inspired by him. I surmise that this distance may be one of the causes of the recent imputations of the Gülen Movement in Germany and the Netherlands.[23]

The Contested Gülen Movement: A Possible Explanation

In his dissertation on the Gülen Movement, Gürkan Çelik mentions three forms of criticism of this movement.[24] The first critique comes from radical Islamists and from ultra-nationalists, and it states that the Gülen Movement undermines Islamic and Turkish identity by seeking dialogue with Christians and Jews. The second critique is leveled at the Gülen Movement from a laicist or secularist point of view, and it says that this movement seeks to undermine the secular nature of the Turkish state by covertly promoting the introduction of Islamic government. The third critique is mainly heard in the West, and it states that this movement deters women from fully participating in its higher ranks.

---

[23] Even though I dislike the term Gülen Movement and prefer the term *Hizmet* (= Service) Movement (see my *Renewing Islam by Service: A Christian View of Fethullah Gülen and the Hizmet Movement,* Washington D.C.: The Catholic University of America Press, 2015), I use "Gülen Movement" in this article because this term, and the suspicions that go with it, is used in the public press media in the Netherlands.

[24] See Gürkan Çelik, *The Gülen Movement: Building Social Cohesion through Dialogue and Education* (Delft: Eburon, 2011).

The form of criticism of the Gülen Movement that caused the Dutch television show "NOVA" to spend 25 minutes on this movement in its broadcast on July 4, 2008 is clearly related to secularist fears of covert Islamism in the movement. The journalist introducing the news broadcast said that a number of scholars of Turkish society think that the Gülen Movement, while pretending to promote dialogue and integration, in fact aims at Islamizing Dutch society. Using government funds, they would indoctrinate students in educational institutions and promote sectarian and separatist behavior. While the Dutch government, in response to questions by parliamentarians after the NOVA broadcast in July 2008 refused to start an investigation of the Gülen Movement, the website of one of the political parties involved later reported that the minister of integration decided to comply with the request to start an investigation of "the movement of the controversial Islamic preacher Fethullah Gülen."[25]

So the question is: How is it possible that an intercultural and interfaith bridge-builder like Fethullah Gülen can be portrayed as a danger for the integration of Turkish Muslims into Dutch society? Those who criticize Gülen and his movement have their answers ready: They say that Gülen has a secret agenda. While posing as bridge-builders, Gülen and his followers are in fact convinced that Islam is the only way to salvation, so they want to expel European freedom of religion and introduce Islamic law instead. Having worked with members of the Gülen Movement for more than 10 years in both the Netherlands and the United States, I do not agree with this imputation. I think that it reflects the secularist Turkish political agenda more than the situation in European countries. At the same time, however, I think that the Gülen Movement shows two characteristics that make it vulnerable to these accusations. These characteristics reflect the situation of extreme tension between a laicist state constitution and a dominant religion in Turkey.

---

[25] See www.sp.nl/integratie. The Dutch government later decided to start a formal investigation, the result of which was published in a report by the Dutch Islamicist Martin van Bruinessen. Nevertheless, questions were asked in Dutch parliament several times and the same suspicions were repeated over and over again. For further developments, see the first chapter in Valkenberg, *Renewing Islam by Service*.

The first characteristic, clearly visible in the NOVA broadcast, is that those who lead a number of organizations that are associated with the Gülen Movement in the Netherlands flatly deny that they have any connection with Gülen. Technically speaking, they might be right because of the loose structure of the Gülen Movement, as demonstrated by Bekim Agai in his research.[26] This does not, however, sound like a convincing argument. It may be dangerous sometimes for Turks, in Turkish society, to admit that they are members of an organization with religious objectives, but in Europe this sounds like denying the obvious especially since the reverence for the person and the thoughts of Fethullah Gülen is noticeable in all media outlets of the movement.

The second characteristic is the already-observed tension between the specific Muslim background in the life and works of Fethullah Gülen and his followers, and the more general type of language in the public aims of the Gülen Movement. It is my opinion that this tension is rooted in the fundamental misconception that one has to suppress one's own religious identity if one wants to contribute to openness and integration of cultures. The life and thoughts of Eboo Patel, quoted at the beginning of this chapter, shows that the opposite is true: You can only be an intercultural and interfaith bridge-builder if you are clear about your specific point of departure. Therefore, I would think that the Gülen Movement would be less vulnerable to the imputation of a double agenda if it could be prouder of its own Islamic identity. The heritage of Desiderius Erasmus could be used to remind the Gülen Movement that Christians and Muslims all have a missionary agenda in the sense that they all want to promote their own faith. But the issue at stake here is that it makes a huge difference whether you do promote your faith by introducing the *shari'ah* and Islamic government or by promoting plurality and cherishing differences. If the movement could acknowledge this point, much could be won. In this respect, I think that it is really true that Christians and Muslims can learn from their differences, and that it is by respecting these differences and by being open about our own faith that we progress in our common quest for the God we seek to serve in this life.

---

[26] Agai, *Zwischen Netzwerk Und Diskurs*

Works Cited

Agai, Bekim. *Zwischen Netzwerk Und Diskurs: Das Bildungsnetzwerk Um Fethullah Gülen (Geb. 1938): Die Flexible Umsetzung Modernen Islamischen Gedankenguts*. Schenefeld: EbVerlag, 2004.

Bange, Patty. "*Dulce Bellum Inexpertis:* Desiderius Erasmus Over Oorlog En Vrede." *Voorlopers In De Vrede* Budel: Damon (2005): 17-30.

Celik, Gurkan, *et al. Voorlopers In De Vrede*. Budel: Damon, 2005.

Celik, Gurkan, and Pim Valkenberg. "Gülen's Approach To Dialogue And Peace: Its Theoretical Background And Some Practical Perspectives." *The International Journal of Diversity in Organisations, Communities & Nations* 7, no. 1, (2007): 29-37.

Çelik, Gürkan, *The Gülen Movement: Building Social Cohesion Through Dialogue And Education*. Delft: Eburon, 2011.

Daniel, Norman. *Islam and the West: The Making of an Image*. Oxford: Oneworld, 1993.

Day, Dorothy. *The Long Loneliness: The Autobiography of the Legendary Catholic Social Activist*. New York: Harpercollins, 1997.

Gioia, Francesco. *Interreligious Dialogue: The Official Teaching of the Catholic Church from the Second Vatican Council to John Paul Ii (1963-2005)*. Boston: Pauline, 2006 Ed.

Goddard, Hugh. *Christians & Muslims: From Double Standards to Mutual Understanding*. London and New York: Routledge Curzon, 1995.

Gülen, Fethullah. *Love and the Essence of Being Human*. Istanbul: Journalists and Writers Foundation, 2004a.

Gülen, Fethullah. *The Necessity of Interfaith Dialog: A Muslim* Perspective. Somerset N.J.: The Light, 2004b.

Gülen, M. Fethullah. *The Statue of Our Souls: Revival in Islamic Activism*. Somerset N.J.: The Light, 2005.

Herwaarden, Jan Van. "Erasmus." *Mevlana En Erasmus*. Amsterdam: Türkevi, (2005): 37-60.

Patel, Eboo. *Acts of Faith: The Story of an American Muslim, the Struggle for the Soul of a Generation*. Boston: Beacon Press, 2007.

Patel, Eboo & Patrice Brodeur. *Building the Interfaith Youth Movement: Beyond Dialogue to Action* Lanham Md: Rowman & Littlefield, 2006, Eds.

Sacks, Jonathan. *The Dignity of Difference: How to Avoid the Clash of* Civilizations. London and New York: Continuum, 2002.

Ünal, Ali, and Alphonse Williams. *Advocate of Dialogue: Fethullah Gülen*. Fairfax: The Fountain, 2000, Comp.

Valkenberg, Pim. *Sharing Lights on the Way to God: Muslim-Christian Dialogue and Theology in the Context of Abrahamic Partnership*. Amsterdam – New York: Rodopi, 2006.

Valkenberg, Pim. *Renewing Islam by Service: A Christian View of Fethullah Gülen and the Hizmet Movement,* Washington D.C.: The Catholic University of America Press, 2015

Williams, Ian. "The Vision of Education within Pluralistic Societies in the Thought of Fethullah Gülen: The Contribution of Non-Denominational Education Towards Inter-Religious and Communal Understanding, Peace and Identity." *Peaceful Coexistence. Fethullah Gülen's Initiatives in the Contemporary World*. London: Leeds Metropolitan University Press. (2007): 407-415.

CHAPTER EIGHT

RELIGIOUS FREEDOM IN THE BAPTIST VISION AND IN FETHULLAH GÜLEN: RESOURCES FOR MUSLIMS AND CHRISTIANS

Paul Weller

I n our globalizing world, how religions respond to diversity is critical for the stability of states and societies, for international relations, and for the future of the religions themselves. In connection with this, religious freedom is an issue that poses challenges to all religions and to many traditional religious approaches and practices, as well as to aspects of modern "secular" ideologies and constitutions. This paper explores the comparisons and contrasts that exist between the Islamic teaching of Fethullah Gülen and the Baptist vision of Christianity with regard to religious freedom. It argues that both are religiously authentic, creative, and corrective resources that can help contemporary Muslims and Christians live in faithful, committed, and peaceful ways in a religiously diverse world.

Fethullah Gülen's Approach and the Baptist Christian Vision

Islam and Christianity are global religions with billions of adherents worldwide. Between them they have an enormous influence that stretches into the cultures, societies, and states that have been shaped by their values. In light of the challenges of our increasingly globalized and pluralized world, how Muslims and Christians understand and practice religious freedom is of critical importance.

From within Christianity, the Baptist tradition is selected for comparison for several reasons. First of all, the Baptist tradition is one of the largest global confessional traditions of Christianity.[1] Secondly, it has generally demonstrated a consistent emphasis on religious liberty. In fact, it is arguable that religious freedom is the closest thing to a "universal" commitment that can be found among Baptists.[2] At the same time, while the Baptist tradition is numerically strongest in the U.S., some parts of the American Baptist tradition — including, most notably, some the forces that are currently dominant within the Southern Baptist Convention in the USA — appear to have lost sight of the importance of the tradition's historical emphasis on religious freedom. The recovery of that emphasis is of great importance, both for the integrity of the Baptist tradition and for its relations with the wider Christian Church and beyond. This chapter refers to the Baptist approach to religious freedom with the descriptor "Baptistic," a term that recognizes the fact that aspects of the historic Baptist vision are shared with other Christian traditions such as Mennonites and other congregationally-based Protestant traditions.

In this chapter, for convenience I will refer to the thinking of Fethullah Gülen and the approaches of those inspired by his teachings as "Gülenian." However, it is important to note that Gülen is not trying to advocate a new or idiosyncratic interpretation of Islam. Rather, his work is concerned with trying to uncover, develop, and apply in a way

---

[1]   Richard Pierard. *Baptists Together in Christ: 1905-2005. A Hundred Year History of the Baptist World Alliance.* (Falls Church, Virginia: Baptist World Alliance, 2005); Ian Randall, Toivo Pilli, and Anthony Cross. "Baptist Identities: International Studies from the Seventeenth to the Twentieth Centuries." *Studies in Baptist History and Thought* 19. (Milton Keynes: Paternoster, 2006).

[2]   Paul Weller. "Freedom and Witness in a Multi-Religious Society: A Baptist Perspective. Part I." *Baptist Quarterly* 33, no. 6, (1990a); Paul Weller. "Freedom and Witness in a Multi Religious Society: a Baptist Perspective. Part II." *Baptist Quarterly* 33, no. 7, (1990b).

appropriate to the contemporary context, an aspect of Islamic tradition that is rooted in the traditional sources of the Qur'an and the Sunnah of the Prophet Muhammad. In addition, acknowledging Sufi influence Gülen stresses that Sufism is the inner dimension of Islam itself and is therefore not to be separated from the Sharia'h.[3]

Historical Roots of Religious Freedom in "Baptistic" Christian Vision

The historical roots of the "Baptistic" Christian vision and its emphasis on religious freedom can probably be traced back to the Anabaptist movements of 16th-century Europe. While there are debated details—such as how the Anabaptist movements relate to the English Separatists—it seems clear that there was at least some creative interchange between the continental Mennonites and the English Separatists who were led by John Smyth and Thomas Helwys. Later, these Separatists founded the first Baptist congregations in England in the early 17th-century.

Baptistic convictions about religious freedom emerged in Europe against a backdrop of the "Wars of Religion" which had resulted in a reactive movement to banish religion into the "private" sphere. In the course of the authoritative survey on *The Development of Religious Toleration in England*, Wilbur Kitchener Jordan argues,

> The great Baptist apologists had made profoundly important contributions to the theory of religious toleration. They had systematised the thought of their predecessors and had broken new ground in their examination of the forces which had for so many centuries made religious devotion synonymous with religious bigotry.[4]

From a religious perspective, the way the Baptistic approach became differentiated can be illustrated with reference to the life of one

---

[3] M. Fethullah Gülen. *Key Concepts in the Practice of Sufism*. (Fairfax, Virginia: The Fountain, 1999).

[4] W.K. Jordan. *The Development of Religious Toleration in England* 1. (London: George Allen and Unwin, 1936): 314.

of the founding Baptists, John Smyth. As Smyth put it in his 1605 *Patterne of True Prayer*, written when he was still a Puritan lecturer in London:

> When there is toleration of many religions, whereby the kingdom of God is shouldered out of doors by the devil's kingdom: for without question the devil is so subtle that he will procure, through the advantage of man's natural inclination to false doctrine and worship, more by thousands to follow strange religions than the truth of God's word: wherefore the magistrates should cause all men to worship the true God, or else punish them with imprisonment, confiscation of goods, or death as the quality of the cause requireth.[5]

From a more political perspective, the position of Edwin Sandys, the Archbishop of York under Queen Elizabeth I, was typical. He argued that religious plurality — even Christian plurality — would inevitably be dangerous to the body politic:

> This liberty, that men may openly profess diversity of religion must needs be dangerous to the Commonwealth. What stirs diversity of religion hath raised in nations and kingdoms the histories are so many and plain, and in our times insuch sort have told you, that with further proof I need not trouble your ears. One God, one King, one profession, is fit for one monarchy and commonwealth. Let conformity and unity in religion be provided for; and it shall be as a wall of defense unto this realm.[6]

In contrast to this is the position taken by the early Baptist Thomas Helwys in his pamphlet addressed to King James I called *The Mistery of Iniquity*, which was the first sustained argument for religious liberty published in the English language. Remarkable for the time, Helwys and other early Baptists did not apply this liberty only to diverse Christian groups, but to everyone: "Let them be heretics, Turks [Muslims],

---

[5] John Smyth. *The Patterne of True Prayer: A Learned and Comfortable Exposition of or Commentarie Upon the Lord's Prayer*, 1605. In: W.T. Whitley (ed.). *The Works of John Smyth* 1. (Cambridge: Cambridge University Press, 1915): 166.

[6] Patrick McGrath. *Papists and Puritans Under Elizabeth I*. (London: Blandford Press, 1967): 1.

Jews, or whatsoever, it appertains not to the earthly power to punish them in the least measure."[7] While this early Baptist commitment to the religious freedom of Jews and Muslims was notable, at the time these groups posed little immediate threat. However, the depth and tenacity of the Baptist commitment can be seen in their determination to include Catholics among those entitled to such freedom. To understand the full significance of the Baptist position in this regard, it must be remembered that English Protestants feared a possible restoration of the Roman Catholic Church that they believed would threaten their own liberty. They also shared in a widespread perception that Catholics were basically disloyal to the country and were thus potential subversives. In light of this, the fact that Baptists remained true to their principles by including Catholics in their stance for religious liberty is convincing evidence about the theological grounding of these convictions.

Significantly, the convictions were also applied to Muslims. In 1660, four Baptists from Kent issued from prison *An Humble Petition and Representation of the Sufferings of Several Peaceable and Innocent Subjects Called by the Name of Anabaptists*. While this publication betrayed a common misunderstanding among Christians of the time that Muslims were worshippers of Muhammad, they also pointed out the absurdity of requiring one's religion to mirror the religion of one's rulers:

> Thus, if we had lived in Turkey we must receive the Koran, and be a worshipper of Mahomet; if in Spain, be a papist; in England, sometimes a papist, as in Henry Eighth's days, a Protestant in Edward Sixth's, a papist again in Queen Mary's, and a Protestant again in Queen Elizabeth's. And so for ever, as the authority changes religion, must we do the same. But God forbid.[8]

---

7   Thomas Helwys. *A Short Declaration of the Mystery of Iniquity*, 1612. In: Richard Groves (ed). *Thomas Helwys: A Short Declaration of the Mystery of Iniquity*. (Macon, Georgia: Mercer University Press, 1998): 53.

8   James Blackmore, George Hammon, William Jeffrey, and John Reve. *An Humble Petition and Representation of the Suffering of Several Peaceable and Innocent Subjects Called by the Name of Anabaptists*, (1616). In Edward Underhill (ed.) *Tracts on the Liberty of Conscience and Persecution, 1614-1667*. (London: Hanserd Knollys Society, 1846): 301.

Historical Roots of Religious Freedom in Gülen's Vision of Islam

What is particularly significant about the clarity and consistency with which Fethullah Gülen's vision of Islam supports and upholds religious freedom — and which Thomas Helwys also propagated — is that this is not the voice of only an individual teacher. Rather, it resonates within a global movement. To fully appreciate its significance, one needs to also understand something about the crucible of modern Turkish history and society out of which it has emerged.

The 20th-century story of Turkey was one that was dominated by the ideology of Mustafa Kemal Ataturk (1881–1938), the founder of the modern Turkish states who abolished the Muslim Caliphate in 1924. Yavuz and Esposito point out that in Kemalist ideology "modernity and democracy require secularism."[9] Indeed, the version of secularism that has been dominant in Turkey is what these authors call a "radical Jacobin liaicism" in which secularism is treated "as above and outside politics" which, therefore, "draws the boundaries of public reasoning." [10] However, Kemalism was established against the background of a traditional Islam that never disappeared from Turkish society. In more recent times, an "Islamist" form of Islam has opposed it. Thus the "Gülenian" vision of Islam is one that that has had to distinguish itself from obscurantist and oppositionist forms of Islam, while also needing to engage with the secular.

In contrast to attempts to enforce either religious or anti-religious stances, Gülen has stated that:

> Efforts to suppress ideas via pressure or brute force have never been truly successful. History shows that no idea was removed by suppressing it. Many great empires and states were destroyed, but an idea or thought whose essence is sound continues to survive."[11]

---

[9] Hakan Yavuz and John Esposito (eds.) *Turkish Islam and the Secular State: The Gülen Movement.* (Syracuse, New York: Syracuse University Press, 2003): xxiii.

[10] Yavuz and Esposito, *Turkish Islam and the Secular State: The Gülen Movement*, xvi

[11] M. Fethullah Gülen. *Towards a Global Civilization of Love and Tolerance.* (Somerset, New Jersey: The Light, 2004): 151-152.

But, according to Gülen, what has always been historically true in this regard is even more the case in our modern, globalized world. As Enes Ergene notes:

> Gülen has stated that in the modern world the only way to get others to accept your ideas is by persuasion. He describes those who resort to force as being intellectually bankrupt; people will always demand freedom of choice in the way they run their affairs and in their expression of their spiritual and religious values.[12]

At the same time, Gülen warns that the transformations which have occurred in our social, historical, institutional, and theological realities may provoke in those who are theologically insecure try to create idealized patterns of life which are, in reality, illusory. For Gülen, the notion that plurality can be abolished is not only illusory, it is also dangerous. Against such dangerous illusions Gülen warns that:

> [D]ifferent beliefs, races, customs, and traditions will continue to cohabit in this village. Each individual is like a unique realm unto themselves; therefore the desire for all humanity to be similar to one another is nothing more than wishing for the impossible. For this reason, the peace of this (global) village lies in respecting all these differences, considering these differences to be part of our nature and in ensuring that people appreciate these differences. Otherwise, it is unavoidable that the world will devour itself in a web of conflicts, disputes, fights, and the bloodiest of wars, thus preparing the way for its own end.[13]

Epistemological and Hermeneutical Roots of Religious Freedom

We have so far noted how the "Gülenian" vision of Islam and the "Baptistic" vision of Christianity can be located in relation to their historical, social, and political roots. However, in order to properly understand the place of religious freedom within both visions, it is important to

---

[12] Gülen, *Towards a Global Civilization of Love and Tolerance*, xii
[13] Gülen, *Towards a Global Civilization of Love and Tolerance*, 249-250

consider that what are today articulated in terms of "human rights" in relation to matters of freedom of religion are, within these religious visions, understood as having profoundly theological roots. Thus, with reference to the closely related notion of "tolerance," Gülen points out that: "First of all, I would like to indicate that tolerance is not something that was invented by us. Tolerance was first introduced on this Earth by the prophets whose teacher was God."[14] Therefore, in the "Gülenian" vision of Islam, tolerance is something that has roots that are much deeper and more constant than mere accidents and expressions of history.

In contrast to shifting intellectual and cultural fashions, the "Gülenian" vision of Islam and the "Baptistic" vision of Christianity understand the world to be rooted in received revelatory truth to which they are called to bear witness, and that reflects the nature of reality as it is. Furthermore, as has been seen through the persecution of Christians and Muslims in different historical and social contexts, the "rootedness" of convictions like these is such that they are unlikely to be undermined — and may even be reinforced — when they encounter various kinds of opposition. In Gülen's vision, he hopes that a "new man and woman" can be developed in which, as he says:

> These new people will be individuals of integrity who, free from external influences, can manage independently of others. No worldly force will be able to bind them, and no fashionable -ism will cause them to deviate from their path. Truly independent of any worldly power, they will think and act freely, for their freedom will be in proportion to their servanthood to God. Rather than imitating others, they will rely on their original dynamics rooted in the depths of history and try to equip their faculties of judgment with authentic values that are their own.[15]

In terms of lifestyle, this leads to an approach to religious plurality in which dialogue and tolerance are key. Gülen clearly outlines what he means by tolerance:

---

[14] Gülen, *Towards a Global Civilization of Love and Tolerance*, 37
[15] Gülen, *Towards a Global Civilization of Love and Tolerance*, 81

> Tolerance does not mean being influenced by others or joining
> them; it means accepting others as they are and knowing how
> to get along with them. No one has the right to say anything
> about this kind of tolerance; everyone in this country has his or
> her own point of view. People with different ideas and thoughts
> are either going to seek ways of getting along by means of rec-
> onciliation or they will constantly fight with one another. There
> have always been people who thought differently to one anoth-
> er and there always will be.[16]

In neither the "Gülenian" vision of Islam nor the "Baptistic" vision
of Christianity is the affirmation of religious freedom — and the promotion of the practice of social and political tolerance that is associated
with this — to be understood in terms of a "liberal" or "modern" adaptation to a plural world consequent upon religion's loss of power or
influence. Rather, it is rooted in a view of religious truth that, ultimately, has confidence in the inherent power of the reality to which truth
claims point.

The "Baptistic" view of religious freedom emerged from within a
Christendom approach to Europe in which religious and civil belonging
was often equated leading to wars in the name of religion. However,
although its pragmatic benefits were recognized, the "Baptistic" vision
does not affirm religious freedom as a product of weariness with religious conflict, or of religious indifferentism, or as a merely pragmatic
approach to the management of religious plurality. In other words, the
"Baptistic" vision was not a "modernist" or "liberal" adjustment to the
advancing tides of "secularization." Rather, it was rooted in a particular
and distinctive understanding of the relationship between human
beings and the divine, and between the community of disciples and
their environment.

For Baptists, that understanding was informed by a specific hermeneutic of the Christian scriptural tradition. Among Baptists, the Christian scriptures have a primacy described by the 18th-century English
Baptist leader Andrew Fuller in terms of his liberation from the shack-
les of an overly dogmatic and narrow Christian tradition. At the begin-

---

[16] Gülen, *Towards a Global Civilization of Love and Tolerance*, 42

ning of 1780, he made a solemn vow in which he declared: "Lord thou hast given me a determination to take up no principle at second-hand; but to search for everything at the pure fountain of thy word."

Such an approach to scripture has also undergirded the general position on creeds that has been found among Christians in the Baptist tradition. In other words, while confessions of faith have been produced around which Baptists have united in particular times and contexts, and while they have traditionally had a "high" view of scripture, there has also been a conviction that the community of believers needs to always engage afresh with the source documents of the Christian tradition in order to discern their relevance in changing contexts. As John Smyth put it when recognizing that the scriptures are not always self-explanatory and that interpretations of them are therefore always open to correction: "We are in constant error; my earnest desire is that my last writing may be taken as my present judgment."[17]

Such a view contrasts, of course, with that of some contemporary Baptist groups such as the current leadership of the Southern Baptist Convention in the U.S., for whom it appears that highly specific interpretations have become requirements that they seek to impose upon others within the same broad tradition.[18] Such an approach is idiosyncratic even with regard to the history of the Convention itself[19] as well as divergent from the broader variety of Baptist tradition in North America.[20] It also contrasts with the vision of the great Southern Baptist theologian, Edgar Mullins, who in his classic book of Baptist theology *The Axioms of Religion*, spoke in a very vivid phrase of the importance of "soul freedom."[21]

---

[17] P. Ballard. *The Dynamic of Independency. The Baptist Quarterly* 23. (1969-70): 245.

[18] Robison James, Gary Leazer, and James Shoopman. *The Fundamentalist Takeover in the Southern Baptist Convention: A Brief History.* (Timisoara: Impact Media, 1999).

[19] Slayden Yarborough. *Southern Baptists: A Historical, Ecclesiological and Theological Heritage of a Confessional People.* (Brentwood, Tennessee: Southern Baptist Historical Society, 2000).

[20] William Brackney. *Baptists in North America: An Historical Perspective.* (Oxford: Blackwell, 2006).

[21] E.Y. Mullins. *The Axioms of Religion.* (Philadelphia: The Judson Press, 1908).

Gülen points out that a similar reification has occurred in parts of the Muslim community. While the "Gülenian" vision of Islam is one that has a high view of the Qur'an, it also has an open and humble posture toward interpretation in relation to which Gülen explains that: "Taking the Qur'an and Sunnah as our main sources and respecting the great people of the past, in the consciousness that we are all children of time, we must question the past and the present."[22] Put straightforwardly, he argues that: "We must review our understanding of Islam." He continues: "I'm looking for laborers of thought and researchers to establish the necessary balance between the unchanging and changing aspects of Islam and, considering such jurisprudential rules as abrogation, particularization, generalization, and restriction, can present Islam to the modern understanding."

Freedom and Witness

In Islam, Muslims are called to "Dawah" in a similar way that, in Christianity, Christians are called to "mission" and/or "evangelism." Modernists among both Muslims and Christians can tend, perhaps for pragmatic reasons, although sometimes on theological grounds, to downplay the universal truth-claims of their respective traditions. At least on the surface, it may seem that a commitment to uphold religious freedom might be fundamentally incompatible with universal claims and desires for dawa/mission. However, in both the "Baptistic" and the "Gülenian" approaches it is the prior and theologically-informed affirmation of religious freedom that enables this to remain a "creative tension" rather than an "impossible contradiction" . It is this affirmation that facilitates the possibility of ethical practice in mission and the freedom of others to accept or reject the invitations. In the "Baptistic" vision of Christianity and the "Gülenian" vision of Islam, the revelations received respectively through the person of Jesus and in the Qur'an are ones to which people of all cultures and religions are invited to respond since revelation is not to be seen as the property of any one group but

---

22 M. Fethullah Gülen. *M. Fethullah Gülen: Essays, Perspectives, Opinions.* (Rutherford, New Jersey: The Light, 2002): 118.

as something received in trust for the whole of humanity. Within this, testimony to what has been received within each religion is believed to take place before God and in dialogue with others whose integrity is affirmed and respected, rather than being an activity that is directed at others in a threatening or manipulative way. Thus, alongside its commitment to religious liberty, the "Baptistic" vision of Christianity has, for much of its history, had a strongly evangelistic commitment. As the 20th-century British Baptist theologian Henry Wheeler-Robinson noted in relation to Baptists:

> It is not an accident of history that they have led the way in foreign missionary work; it is a logical and obvious deduction from their emphasis on individual faith. The measure of personal conviction is seen in its vigor of expansion, its zeal of propagation.

At the same time, Wheeler-Robinson was clear that "we cannot reverse this and say that where there is propagating zeal, there is the Christian conviction of a world-gospel, because many other motives may lead men to become zealous proselytizers." Indeed, there have always been those who have engaged in forms of mission that work counter to the nature of the message with which the they have been entrusted. But in the "Gülenian" vision of Islam, while Muslims are still called upon to manifest the revelation of God in the world, Gülen teaches that:

> [A]n Islamic goal can be achieved only through Islamic means and methods. Muslims must pursue Islamic goals and adopt Islamic methods to attain them. As God's approval cannot be obtained without sincerity and a pure intention, Islam cannot be served and Muslims cannot be directed toward their real targets through diabolic means and methods."[23]

Therefore, what is needed among both Muslims and Christians is a theological system of ethics that bears witness to the revelatory truth

---

[23] Ali Ünal and Alphonse Williams (eds.) *Advocate of Dialogue*. (Fairfax, Virginia: The Fountain, 2000): 99.

that each claims to have received, but which translates into a style of faithful living among others in which modesty and integrity are combined with realism and distinctiveness. This gives people of all religions and no religion the social and theological space to witness to their own understanding of truth as well as to be free to respond to what is shared with them. It means that real witness is always dialogical, and because of such an understanding, particular theological ethics are implicit in a "Baptistic" and a "Gülenian" approach to religious believing and belonging. Indeed, if the theological ethics of religious freedom are not merely an addendum to the basic tasks of Christianity and Islam, then the praxis of inter-religious dialogue must be understood as part of a transformative understanding of truth.

Because of this, it is possible even for committed believers in one religion to benefit not only from the cognate ideas of others, but even from opposing ideas. As Gülen expresses it, "We should have so much tolerance that we can benefit from opposing ideas in that they force us to keep our heart, spirit, and conscience active and aware, even if these ideas do not directly or indirectly teach us anything."[24] Significantly, this approach to dialogue does not remain at the level of teaching alone. Rather, it is expressed through symbolic and effective action. As Bekim Agai explains it:

> Although many Islamic leaders may talk of tolerance in Islam, it may be problematic to put it into practice. Gülen himself has shown that he has no fears of meeting leaders of other religions, including the Pope and the representative of the Jewish community in Istanbul. He also crossed the borders of Islamic discourse to meet with important people in Turkish society who are atheists. These activities were not easy from a religious perspective because Islamic discourse in Turkey has definite boundaries that do not appreciate close ties to the leaders of other religions and nonreligious persons. Also, his support for the Alevis was not very popular among most Sunni-Islamic groups.[25]

---

[24] Gülen, *Towards a Global Civilization of Love and Tolerance*, 33
[25] Bekim Agai. *The Gülen Movement's Islamic Ethic of Education*. In Hakan Yavuz and John Esposito (eds.) *Turkish Islam and the Secular State: The Gülen Movement*. (Syracuse, New York: Syracuse University Press, 2003): 65.

What this dialogical approach also means in relation to "secular" people can be seen especially clearly in the work of the Journalists and Writers' Foundation and of its so-called Abant Platform in which challenging topics for the Turkish context have been addressed such as "Islam and Secularism" and "Pluralism and Social Reconciliation." Fethullah Gülen is the President of the Foundation while, since 2006, its Academic Coordinator of the Abant Platform has been Professor Dr. Mete Tuncay of Bilgi University — who refers to himself as agnostic. In this and other similar ways, the spirit of dialogue and the theologically grounded freedom to believe or not to believe, is embodied in both action and organization.

Religious Freedom, the State, and Civil Society

At around the time that "Baptistic" forms of Christianity originally emerged in European history, there were also those on the radical wing of the Reformation who wanted to try to use the Hebrew Scriptures as a template for the establishment of a civil community they believed could embody the biblical vision of justice and righteousness. In contrast to such a totalizing vision of the relationship between religion, state, and society, "Baptistic" Christians have generally held to a conviction that the scriptures are to be interpreted according to a predominantly Christological and soteriological hermeneutic. This approach accorded a relative primacy to the writings of the New Testament and was at least partly responsible for leading Baptists away from an attempt to recreate the theocratic patterns of the Hebrew Scriptures.

Such an approach rested upon the prior theological conviction about the importance of religion as a freely chosen life orientation and commitment. In providing a basis for seeking the restoration of what was believed to be a New Testament pattern of church life it also reinforced a differentiation between the church and the social order, leading to a different kind of approach to being Christian in society and the state. Thus, Thomas Helwys argued that religious coercion could become an excuse for people to try to circumvent their individual responsibility and conscience. He also believed magistrates and kings committed a grave sin when they forced the conscience of an individual or group. Because of this, in his *Mistery of Iniquity*, he eloquently argued:

> O Let the King judge is it not most equal, that men should choose their religion themselves seeing they only must stand themselves before the judgment seat of God to answer for themselves, when it shall be no excuse for them to say, we were commanded or compelled to be of this religion, by the king, or by them that had authority from him.[26]

Helwys paid for his courage and convictions with the loss of his liberty and finally with his life. However, other Baptists soon followed his early advocacy of religious liberty. In 1614, Leonard Busher published a pamphlet entitled *Religion's Peace*,[27] the title of which continued with the words: "Wherein is Contained Certain Reasons against Persecution for Religion: Also a design for a peaceable reconciling of those that differ in opinion." In this, Busher argued that "if the believing should persecute the unbelieving to death, who should remain alive?"[28]

This was followed in 1620 by *An Humble Supplication to the King, Prince Charles and the Parliament*,[29] which was thought to be authored by John Murton. Roger Williams, who became a Baptist and founded the first Baptist church in North America, used Murton's pamphlet as a preface to his own 1644 classic work on religious liberty, *The Bloudy Tenent of Persecution for Cause of Conscience Discussed in a Conference Between Truth and Peace*.[30] Williams maintained in uncompromising words that:

---

[26] Helwys, *A Short Declaration of the Mystery of Iniquity*, 37

[27] Leonard Busher. *Religion's Peace: Or a Plea for Liberty of Conscience*, (1614). In Edward Underhill (ed.) *Tracts on the Liberty of Conscience and Persecution, 1614-1667*. (London: Hanserd Knollys Society, 1846): 1-81.

[28] Busher, *Religion's Peace: Or a Plea for Liberty of Conscience*, 21

[29] Busher, *Religion's Peace: Or a Plea for Liberty of Conscience*, 189-231

[30] Roger Williams, 1664. In Richard Groves. (ed.) *The Bloudy Tenent of Persecution for Cause of Conscience Discussed in a Conference Between Truth and Peace*. Macon, Georgia: Mercer University Press.

> [I]t is the will and command of God that, since the coming of his Son, the Lord Jesus, a permission of the most Paganish, Jewish, Turkish, or anti-Christian consciences and worships be granted to all men in all nations and countries: and that they are to be fought against with the sword which is only, in soul matters, able to conquer: to wit, the sword of God's spirit, the word of God.[31]

In terms of both theology and the practicalities of state, Williams argued that "true civility and Christianity may both flourish in a state or kingdom, notwithstanding the permission of diverse and contrary consciences, either of Jew or Gentile."[32] By contrast, Williams maintained that "an enforced uniformity of religion throughout a nation or a civil state confounds the civil and religious, denies the principles of Christianity and civility, and that Jesus Christ is come in the flesh."

Just as the early "Baptistic" Christian teachers challenged a totalizing religious vision of Christianity, so Gülen also challenges contemporary "Islamist" visions of Islam. Thus, while noting that, "Supposedly there are Islamic regimes in Iran and Saudi Arabia," Gülen goes on to say that these "are state-determined and limited to sectarian approval."[33] Both traditionalist and contemporary "Islamist" Muslims highlight a tension, if not outright incompatibility, between what is identified as *dar al-harb* (territory that lays outside the sway of Islam) and what is called *dar al-Islam* (those lands within which Islam has taken root). However, others — of which Ihsan Yilmaz sees the community associated with Gülen's teaching as an example — are more concerned with what Yilmaz, after Gülen, identifies as *dar ul-hizmet* (country of service).[34]

Such an approach presents an alternative to instrumentalization of religion in the service of politics or politics in the service of religion, and emphasizes instead an understanding of the contribution to public life which service based on religious motivations can make, but as one

[31] Williams, *The Bloudy* Tenent, 3
[32] Williams, *The Bloudy* Tenent, 4
[33] Gülen, *Towards a Global Civilization of Love and Tolerance*, 151
[34] Ihsan Yilmaz, 2002

contribution alongside others. As Bulent Aras and Omer Caha summarize it:

> Gülen's movement seems to have no aspiration to evolve into a political party or seek political power. On the contrary, Gülen continues a long Sufi tradition of seeking to address the spiritual needs of people, to educate the masses, and to provide some stability in times of turmoil. Like many previous Sufi figures (including the towering thirteenth-century figure, Jalal al-Din Rumi), he is wrongly suspected of seeking political power. However, any change from this apolitical stance would very much harm the reputation of his community.[35]

In this regard, the Gülenian vision again proves itself to be very close to the "Baptistic" vision in that both have challenged any form of a religion-state relationship in which either religion or state are instrumentalized in the service of the other, or in which temporal structures are held to approximate to a divine blueprint.

Such a stance was what led to the 19th-century Baptist Union in England becoming a founding member group of the British Anti-State Church Association, later known as the Liberation Society. The more formal and longer name of the Society — the Society for the Liberation of the Church from State Patronage and Control — emphasized that while the "establishment" of one form of Christianity was seen as being detrimental to the state and society, it was also considered damaging to true religion. This has generally been the position Baptists have held in most times and places, and is today also being updated and reinterpreted with reference to contemporary plural societies.[36] Once again, in this there are strong resonances with the teaching of Fethullah Gülen who argues that:

> Politicizing religion would be more dangerous for religion than for the regime, for such people want to make politics a means for all their ends. Religion would grow dark within them, and

---

[35] Bulent Aras and Omer Caha, (2000): 30
[36] Paul Weller. *Time for a Change: Reconfiguring Religion, State and Society.* (London: T&T Clark, 2005).

they would say: "We are the representatives of religion." This is a dangerous matter. Religion is the name of the relationship between humanity and God, which everyone can respect.[37]

Indeed, in Gülen, one can also hear echoes of Thomas Helwys who, in his *Mistery of Iniquity*, challenged King James I:

Our Lord the King is but an earthly king and he hath no authority as a King but in earthly causes, and if the King's people be obedient and true subjects, obeying all humane laws made by the King, our Lord the King can require no more: for men's religion to God, is betwixt God and themselves: the King shall not answer for it, neither may the King be judge between God and man.[38]

Of course, there is an opposite danger to totalizing visions of religion, state, and society, which is that of a pietistic withdrawal from the structures and processes of civil society, and especially of governance, and to concentrate on personal religious life in the family and among like-minded religious people.

In relation to the "Baptistic" tradition of Christianity, pietistic withdrawal from the world has become more common among Baptists today, but historically, it was more characteristic of certain parts of the "Anabaptist" tradition, illustrated by the major divergence that "Anabaptists" and "Baptists" had over the office of the magistracy. The Anabaptist position was generally that a member of the Christian community could not hold the office of magistrate because it implied the use of the force, which Anabaptists viewed as contrary to the Gospel imperative for leaving judgment to God. Baptists, on the other hand, allowed their members to be magistrates, while maintaining that they should not thereby become agents of compulsion in matters of conscience. By not seeing what they called "the sword" of magisterial responsibility as incompatible with membership of the Christian church, Baptists affirmed the importance of the involvement of Christians in matters of social and structural responsibility.

---

37 Ünal and Williams, *Advocate of Dialogue*, 166
38 Helwys, *A Short Declaration of the Mystery of Iniquity*, 53

In relation to Islam, it is clear that the "Gülenian" approach contrasts strongly with that of those Muslims who would wish either to establish an Islamic theocracy in a particular country — such as Iran under the Mullahs, Afghanistan under the Taliban, or the Caliphate of Isis. Many Sufis advocated a different approach, but given the way modern Turkish history systematically excludes religion not only from the political sphere, but also from education and other key sectors of civil society, the consequence was sometimes that of a withdrawal from society.

In contrast, Gülen has argued for a full engagement with the world, which enables Gülen to take the position, as reported by Yavuz, that "Islam does not need the state to survive, but rather needs educated and financially rich communities to flourish. In a way, not the state but rather community is needed under a full democratic system."[39] Against the background of a Turkish system in which military coups have several times cut across the democratic process, Enes Ergene has pointed out that Gülen has come to a position in which he argues that:

> Democracy ... in spite of its many shortcomings, is now the only viable political system, and people should strive to modernize and consolidate democratic institutions in order to build a society where individual rights and freedoms are respected and protected, where equal opportunity for all is more than a dream.[40]

Gülen continues: "Democracy is a system of freedoms. However, because we have to live together with our different positions and views, our freedom is limited where that of another begins."[41] Furthermore, with reference to his vision of a "Golden Generation," Gülen argues, "The generation that will become responsible for bringing justice and happiness to the world should be able to think freely and

[39] Hakan Yavuz. *Turkey's Puritans*, (2003). In Hakan Yavuz and John Esposito (eds.) *Turkish Islam and the Secular State: The Gülen Movement.* (Syracuse, New York: Syracuse University Press): 45.
[40] Gülen, *Towards a Global Civilization of Love and Tolerance*, xii
[41] Gülen, *Towards a Global Civilization of Love and Tolerance*, 151

respect freedom of thought. Freedom is a significant dimension of human free will and a key to the mysteries of human identity."[42]

"Gülenian" and "Baptistic" Contributions in a Plural and Global Society

The "Baptistic" refraction of the Christian vision could make a "radical methodological contribution to the basis on which the theology and practice of inter-religious dialogue is usually constructed"[43] among Christians. The potential radicalism of the Baptist contribution is not because of its adaptation to the modern world, but precisely because of its fidelity and authenticity in relation to the foundational vision of Christianity. It is the argument of this essay that a similarly radical methodological contribution can be made for Islam and Muslims through the "Gülenian" vision of Islam, rooted as it is in its fidelity to the Qur'an and Sunnah, drawing upon the rich synthesis developed in the Turkish appropriation of Islam, and translating that into action via a community of transformative action and a pattern of civil initiatives.

While this essay has sought to stress the theological roots of these religious visions of religious freedom, it is interesting that in Leonard Busher's *Religion's Peace*, alongside the arguments that he made on theological and ecclesiological grounds, he also challenged Christians with historical descriptions of the Muslim treatment of Christians and Jews in Constantinople. In his pamphlet Busher writes,

> I read that a bishop of Rome would have constrained a Turkish emperor to the Christian faith, unto whom the emperor answered, "I believe that Christ was an excellent prophet, but he did never, so far as I understand, command that men should, with the power of weapons be constrained to believe his law: and verily I also do force no man to Mahomet's law." And I read that Jews, Christians, and Turks are tolerated in Constantinople, and yet are peaceable, though so contrary the one to the other.[44]

---

[42] Gülen, *Towards a Global Civilization of Love and Tolerance*, 99

[43] Weller, "Freedom and Witness in a Multi-Religious Society: a Baptist Perspective. Part II," 314

[44] Busher, *Religion's Peace: Or a Plea for Liberty of Conscience*, 24

From citing this practical example, Busher went on to use it in order to press the point by comparison upon the Christians of his time that:

> If this be so, how much more ought Christians not to force on another to religion. AND HOW MUCH MORE OUGHT CHRISTIANS TO TOLERATE CHRISTIANS, WHEN THE TURKS DO TOLERATE THEM? SHALL WE BE LESS MERCIFUL THAN THE TURKS? OR SHALL WE LEARN THE TURKS TO PERSECUTE CHRISTIANS? IT IS NOT ONLY UNMERCIFUL, BUT UNNATURAL AND ABOMINABLE. YEA, MONSTROUS FOR ONE CHRISTIAN TO VEX AND DESTROY ANOTHER FOR DIFFERENCE AND QUESTIONS OF RELIGION.[45]

Bearing this in mind, it is interesting to read what M. Enes Ergene has to say in relation to the linkage between this historical inheritance and the "Gülenian" approach. As the author of the foreword to Gülen's book, *Towards a Global Civilization of Love and Tolerance*, Ergen explains that Gülen's model is "the essence of the synthesis created by the coming together of Turkish culture with Islam"; that "this tolerance was initiated by Muslim Turkish Sufis"; and that "Muslim Turks have practiced tolerance and concurrence, which are the essence of the contemporary democracy, over a vast geography for centuries. Islam has been interpreted in this geography with the same tolerance for a thousand years."[46]

Therefore, like the original "Baptistic" visions of Christianity, Fethullah Gülen's vision of Islam is not that of a "modernist" or "liberal" project that could easily be dismissed as a betrayal of true Islam by Muslims who have a more theocratic approach to the relationship between religion, state, and society. Rather, based on his wide and deep knowledge of Muslim, and especially of Ottoman history, Gülen's approach is one of a tajdid or "renewal" of Islam that is rooted in the common Islamic sources of the Qur'an and Sunnah, but it also seeks positive engagement with the contemporary world and, within that,

---

[45] Capitalization in original

[46] Gülen, *Towards a Global Civilization of Love and Tolerance*, 7

with people of all religions and no religion. As Ergen explains it, Gülen's model is one that "regenerates this tolerant interpretation and understanding of Muslim-Turkish Sufism within contemporary circumstances, albeit highlighting a broader, more active, and more socially oriented vision ... Gülen opens up this framework and vision to all societies in the world, transforming and broadening it."[47]

Conclusion

In conclusion, this essay emphasizes the importance of religious freedom in the contemporary world as part of a global framework of human rights, but it also argues that if the reality of religious freedom is to be both deepened and extended, it is important that this is done not only "externally" to the religious traditions of the world through "secular" reasoning and the instruments of international law, but also that it is developed in articulation with the "logic" and the "grammar" of the religions of the religions themselves.

Within Christianity, the particular refraction of the Christian vision that can be found in the "Baptistic" tradition's commitment to religious freedom offers historical, ecclesiological, and theological resources that can help to equip the wider Christian community for a future in which Christians can understand and grapple with the challenges posed by the religious plurality of the contemporary world, not only in terms of toleration, but also as an expression of a deeply theological commitment.

Within Islam, the teaching of Fethullah Gülen and the practice of the movement that looks for inspiration to his teaching have emerged out of a clash within Turkish history between a radical and often antireligious form of "secularism" and obscurantist and/or oppositionist forms of being Muslim. It draws on the best elements of the Ottoman-Turkish inheritance with regard to toleration. However, it has also issued into a global vision of Islamic integrity in its commitment to religious freedom that is deeply rooted in the Qur'an and the Sunnah, while being fully and dialogically engaged with the plurality of the contemporary world.

---

[47] Gülen, *Towards a Global Civilization of Love and Tolerance*, viii

Works Cited

Agai, Bekim. *The Gülen Movement's Islamic Ethic of Education*. In Hakan Yavuz and John Esposito (eds.) *Turkish Islam and the Secular State: The Gülen Movement*. Syracuse, New York: Syracuse University Press, 2003: 48-68.

Ballard, P. *The Dynamic of Independency*. The Baptist Quarterly *23* (1969-70): 241-250.

Blackmore, James, George Hammon, William Jeffrey, and John Reve. *An Humble Petition and Representation of the Suffering of Several Peaceable and Innocent Subjects Called by the Name of Anabaptists*. (1616). In Edward Underhill (ed.) *Tracts on the Liberty of Conscience and Persecution, 1614-1667*. London: Hanserd Knollys Society, 1846: 287 308.

Brackney, William. *Baptists in North America: An Historical Perspective*. Oxford: Blackwell, 2006.

Busher, Leonard. *Religion's Peace: Or a Plea for Liberty of Conscience*, (1614). In Edward Underhill (ed.) *Tracts on the Liberty of Conscience and Persecution, 1614-1667*. London: Hanserd Knollys Society, 1846: 1-81.

Gülen, M. Fethullah. *Key Concepts in the Practice of Sufism*. Fairfax, Virginia: The Fountain, 1999).

Gülen, M. Fethullah. *M. Fethullah Gülen: Essays, Perspectives, Opinions*. Rutherford, New Jersey: The Light, 2002.

Gülen, M. Fethullah. *Towards a Global Civilization of Love and Tolerance*. Somerset, New Jersey: The Light, 2004.

Groves, Richard. (ed). *Thomas Helwys: A Short Declaration of the Mystery of Iniquity*. Macon, Georgia: Mercer University Press, 1998.

Groves, Richard. (ed). *Roger Williams: The Bloudy Tenent of Persecution for Cause of Conscience Discussed in a Conference Between Truth and Peace*. Macon, Georgia, Mercer University Press.

Helwys, Thomas. *A Short Declaration of the Mystery of Iniquity*, 1612. In: Richard. Groves (ed). *Thomas Helwys: A Short Declaration of the Mystery of Iniquity*. Macon, Georgia: Mercer University Press, 1998.

James, Robison, Gary Leazer, and James Shoopman. *The Fundamentalist Takeover in the Southern Baptist Convention: A Brief History*. Timisoara: Impact Media, 1999.

Jordan, W.K. *The Development of Religious Toleration in England* 1. London: George Allen and Unwin, 1936.

McGrath, Patrick. *Papists and Puritans Under Elizabeth I.* London: Blandford Press, 1967.

Mullins, E.Y. *The Axioms of Religion.* Philadelphia: The Judson Press, 1908.

Pierard, Richard. *Baptists Together in Christ: 1905-2005. A Hundred Year History of the Baptist World Alliance.* Falls Church, Virginia: Baptist World Alliance, 2005.

Randall, Ian, Toivo Pilli, and Anthony Cross. "Baptist Identities: International Studies from the Seventeenth to the Twentieth Centuries." *Studies in Baptist History and Thought* 19. Milton Keynes: Paternoster, 2006.

Smyth, John. *The Patterne of True Prayer: A Learned and Comfortable Exposition of or Commentarie Upon the Lord's Prayer,* 1605. In: W.T. Whitley (ed.). *The Works of John Smyth* 1. Cambridge: Cambridge University Press, 1915.

Ünal, Ali and Alphonse Williams. (eds.) *Advocate of Dialogue.* Fairfax, Virginia: The Fountain, 2000.

Weller, Paul. "Freedom and Witness in a Multi-Religious Society: A Baptist Perspective. Part I." *Baptist Quarterly* 33, no. 6, (1990a): 252-264

Weller, Paul. "Freedom and Witness in a Multi-Religious Society: a Baptist Perspective. Part II." *Baptist Quarterly* 33, no. 7, (1990b): 302-315.

Weller, Paul. *Time for a Change: Reconfiguring Religion, State and Society.* London: T&T Clark, 2005.

Weller, Paul. "Human rights, religion and the secular: variant configurations of religion(s), state(s) and society(ies)." *Religion and Human Rights: An International Journal* 1, no. 1, (2006): 17-39.

Williams, Roger, 1664. In Groves, Richard. (ed.) *The Bloudy Tenent of Persecution for Cause of Conscience Discussed in a Conference Between Truth and Peace.* Macon, Georgia: Mercer University Press.

Yarborough, Slayden. *Southern Baptists: A Historical, Ecclesiological and Theological Heritage of a Confessional People.* Brentwood, Tennessee: Southern Baptist Historical Society, 2000.

Yavuz, Hakan. *Turkey's Puritans,* 2003. In Hakan Yavuz and John Esposito (eds.) *Turkish Islam and the Secular State: The Gülen Movement.* Syracuse, New York: Syracuse University Press: 19-47.

Yavuz, Hakan and Esposito, John. (eds.) *Turkish Islam and the Secular State: The Gülen Movement.* Syracuse, New York: Syracuse University Press, 2003.

CHAPTER NINE

DIALOGUE BETWEEN JESUIT AND GÜLEN EDUCATIONAL AND SPIRITUAL FOUNDATIONS

Patrick J. Howell

I n 1601, an Italian Jesuit missionary named Matteo Ricci reached the outskirts of the Mandarin Court in Beijing. He quietly exchanged his clerical, European garb for silk robes and a Chinese fedora to signify his status as a scholar to the Beijing elite. This simple gesture marked an important feature of Jesuit education, namely, to adapt Jesuit spirituality and faith to the local culture and to engage the best aspirations of the people that the Jesuits encountered.

In a similar manner, Fethullah Gülen and the movement originating in Turkey that he inspired have adapted the fundamental insights of Sufi Islam to dialogue with and engage the best aspirations of contemporary people and cultures. His world-vision provides a foundation for inspired education in diverse cultures today.

This essay will attempt to compare and contrast Jesuit education and its foundational spirituality with the Turkish education inspired by the Turkish philosopher Fethullah Gülen, who reconciled Islam and its Sufi expression to contemporary culture and its aspirations, whether in Turkey or elsewhere.

The Spiritual Inspiration for Jesuit and Gülen Education[1]

Both Ignatius of Loyola and Fethullah Gülen, though centuries apart, drew on profound religious experiences and spiritual insight to articulate their experiences of God and their visions for life. Given the vast impact of both men, I will explore only three salient religious features of each man and then how their spiritual insights and practices played such a strong impact on the educational enterprises that arose from their respective visions. These three features include: 1) their mystical and religious roots, 2) their emphasis on experience and pragmatic *action*, rather than a retreat from daily life; 3) and their devotion to building up *community*. After exploring these three dimensions, I will suggest the implications of these religious roots for each of the educational traditions that have sprung forward with such amazing impact and effectiveness. At the end of each of these three sections, I will also propose some questions for ongoing dialogue between Jesuit education and Gülen education.[2] Before I examine these three features, however, some general background on both Ignatius of Loyola and Fethullah Gülen, as well as their followers, will be helpful.

---

[1]   I am using "Gülen tradition" and "Gülen education" for the more correct, but awkward term of "Gülen-inspired" tradition or "Gülen-inspired" education. Gülen himself disclaims any intention of founding a movement or an educational "system." It may take time for appropriate terminology to emerge. In Jesuit parlance, one can say "Ignatian spirituality" or "Ignatian pedagogy," but not "Ignatian education." The term "Jesuit" was first used by the enemies of the Society of Jesus who thought it was arrogant and presumptuous for the companions of Ignatius to name themselves after "Jesus."

[2]   Disclaimer: Having been a Jesuit for the last 48 years and having taught in Jesuit secondary schools and universities for 37 of those years, I am thoroughly acquainted with Jesuit spiritual and educational traditions. But my acquaintance with Gülen and Gülen-inspired education is extremely recent. In May 2008, sponsored by the Acacia Foundation (Seattle), I traveled to Turkey with a group of Christian-Muslim-Jewish leaders and was immensely impressed by the hospitality, generosity, and religious devotion of the Turkish groups, inspired and vitalized by the teachings of Gülen.

Context and Background

Profoundly aware of his own transformative path, Ignatius of Loyola provided a road map in a little book called *The Spiritual Exercises* to guide others seeking God's will and providential love in their lives. The guidebook embodied a vision of the Incarnation, that is, of the Son of God becoming human and entering more and more concretely into the human struggle and engagement in all dimensions of the world. It provided a manual for spiritual guidance to free a person from predispositions and biases, thus enabling one to make free choices. It was based on the premise that people who are free enough to see reality as good will recognize their own goodness and will live happy and fulfilled lives. Simultaneously, they will see the goodness of all other human beings and seek to live in harmony and peace, building up the "Kingdom of God," which is the realization of peace and justice both in this life and the next.

The genius and innovation Ignatius brought to education flowed directly from his religious vision embodied in the *Spiritual Exercises* and from his own education at the University of Paris, among the top four or five universities of its day.

Loyola's Jesuit companions and followers were steeped in the Renaissance, in its resurgent humanism and the latest in science. Often outstanding scholars themselves, they inspired their students with the new humanism linked to their Catholic faith and created a model of education replicated throughout Europe. The foundation for this Jesuit education was the path of self-discovery laid out in *The Exercises* by Ignatius.

Unlike Fethullah Gülen, Ignatius himself never developed a coherent, overarching philosophy. Instead he provided guidance, instruction, and institutional support for people seeking God and deciding how they could be of the greatest service to others. The full articulation of Jesuit education came only 44 years after the death of Ignatius (1556) and after much experience and experimentation by the early Jesuits (1551-1601).

Only after several decades of experimentation did the Jesuits finalize a *Ratio Studio-rum,* a "program of studies" for all their schools. By 1601 the early Jesuits had reached out to all the known corners of the globe, establishing schools in such diverse places as Peru, Paraguay, Goa, Prague, Lisbon, Messina (Sicily), and Cologne. They adapted themselves to the local customs, learned the native language, often wrote the first dictionaries for native peoples without a written language, and, within certain limitations, they created communities of learning and sought to dialogue with scholars and all people of faith.

The goal of Jesuit education has always been to enable its students and alumni to achieve an "educated solidarity" with the poor and oppressed, to be more concerned about their fellow human beings. It helps direct youth to find God and to grow in appreciation of the arts to value beauty, grammar to learn how to read, rhetoric to express oneself, mathematics to enable one to think, and theology and philosophy to find God.[3] Perhaps this experiential model of development can be instructive to the Gülen-inspired schools — namely, that if they are going to last and be effective, it will be helpful to develop well-articulated resources, networks, and exchange of "best practice" so that the initial foundations can flourish and spread even more than they have already. A concomitant danger, of course, is that the institutionalization phase in Gülen education risks the dangers of losing the founder's charisma, especially after the founder and the initial circle of friends or supporters have died off.

The contemporary Turkish philosopher Fethullah Gülen (1941 -) has had a tremendous, inspirational effect on education throughout the world. His philosophy draws on the rich Islamic tradition expressed in Sufism to offer a contemporary, inspirational way of life and action. Gülen believes that fusing religious belief and scientific education enables a person to better understand the mysteries of the world and the Creator's revelation of Himself to humanity. "The foundation of [Gülen's] message consists of joining religious belief and modern scientific education to create a better world, one based on positive activism,

---

3   See www.holycross.edu/jesuit/traditions

altruism, interfaith, and intercultural dialogue, and a desire to serve others and thereby gain God's good pleasure."[4]

Gülen has spent his life helping people to understand that true religion advocates love, tolerance, open-mindedness, compassion, hard work, and peace that lead a person to virtue and perfection. Early in his career, Gülen traveled throughout the Turkish provinces and lectured in mosques, town meeting halls, and corner coffee houses, attracting the attention especially of students and teachers. His talks encompassed a wide range of subjects: religious matters, education, science, Darwinism, the economy, and social justice. He urged his audiences to search for the truth by balancing material and spiritual values. He attempted to synthesize positive science with religion and to bring the ideologies and philosophies of East and West closer together.[5] He encouraged young people to harmonize intellectual enlightenment with wise spirituality and a caring, humane activism.

Gülen has been a driving force to establish schools worldwide to provide a balanced, well-rounded education of tomorrow's professionals by equipping students with knowledge and skills, as well as sound moral/ethical values. He has dedicated his life to educating the heart, soul, and mind to invigorate the whole being of each person so that they can become competent in their own specialty, and thus be of service to others. The Gülen schools focus on modern and scientific education. Religious matters are completely absent from their curricula. In all these countries, as a consequence of the Soviet legacy and of the local leaders' suspicion, religion has no place in the educational system. The Jesuits have had a similar strategy in its schools in Iraq, Nepal, and other countries, where Islam, Hinduism, or some other religion is pervasive. In these circumstances, they allowed no proselytizing, and no religion was taught.

Ultimately Gülen believes that the 21st century will witness the birth of a spiritual dynamic that will revitalize long-dormant moral

---

4   Fethullah Gülen, *M.F. Gülen: Essays, Perspectives, Opinions*, (Rutherford, NJ: The Light, Inc.2002), foreword.

5   Gülen, *M.F. Gülen*, 4-5

values. He foresees an age of tolerance, understanding, and international cooperation ultimately leading to a single inclusive civilization based on intercultural dialogue and the sharing of values.

The Gülen movement's schools are managed by Turkish and national administrators and teachers. Usually scientific matters (e.g. biology, physics, and computer science) are the main courses and are taught in English and Turkish languages. The particular national language is also very much present.

No one knows exactly the size of Gülen's enormous community of followers and sympathizers. A number of years ago the estimate was about 3 million members; today it numbers at more than 5 million members.[6] The movement obtains much of its support from young urban men, especially doctors, academics, and other professionals. The movement has grown in part by sponsoring student dormitories, summer camps, colleges, universities, classrooms, and communication organizations. Without any doubt, education is central to the identity of the community and favored its growth in the Balkans, Central Asia, and the Turkic world in general. The Central Asian Turkic Republics enjoy a special position in Gülen's strategy. Gülen's early connections with these Turkic Republics of the former Soviet Union helped to inaugurate dozens of schools. Statistics show that in January 2001, for instance, the movement in Kazakhstan already had 30 high schools and one university, welcoming 5,664 pupils and employing 580 teachers from Turkey. Similar success was achieved in Kyrgyzstan, Turkmenistan, and Uzbekistan.[7]

From the outset it seems that Ignatius of Loyola (1491-1556) and Fethullah Gülen could not be more different. Ignatius comes from a 16th-century, Spanish Christian Kingdom that had recently expelled the Moors and the Jews from Spain, while Gülen was born in Erzurum in eastern Turkey in 1941, three years after Atatürk, the secular founder of Turkey, died.

---

[6] Alain Woodrow, "Islam's Moderate Pioneers," *The Tablet* (2009): 14-15.
[7] A summary of the "Gülen movement" in education can be found on *Religionscope* at http://www. religion.info/ (April 2002).

Ignatius was an itinerant 16th-century pilgrim searching for an adequate education for a decade before graduating from the University of Paris. Already 36 when he finished his advanced studies, Ignatius relished the rich store of Renaissance humanism and medieval philosophy he had experienced, but his entire *raison d'être* was "helping souls," enabling them to become the best they were called to be by their Creator. Gülen, on the other hand, was a well-educated 20th-century Islamic cleric, who began his career as an official preacher for the government in 1963. In 1966, the director of religious affairs sent him to Izmir, where he organized a community with a small group of students and businessmen. Gülen sought a new pathway by drawing deeply on the tenets of Sufism, contemporary philosophy, and the needs of 20th-century Turkish society.

Sufism is a life-long process of spiritual development. Each state or station attained through this process is a gift from God, for which an individual must actively prepare him or herself to receive. In his book on *Sufism*, Gülen describes this life-long journey. In fact, what he provides is a series of meditations on spiritual virtues and challenges. These include, for example, freedom (*Hurriya*), altruism (I'thar), knowledge ('*ilm*), wisdom (*Hikma*), discernment (*Firasa*), passion (*Qalaq*), abstinence (*Wara'*), ecstasy (*Wajd*), and willful rapture (*Tawajud*) — 48 topics in all, which of course, makes it impossible to summarize them in a short essay such as this. For the Western reader such as myself, one suspects that these meditations resemble a modern-day book of Proverbs — highly poetic with great spiritual depth — and that they would resonate more profoundly and deeply with those reading them in the original Turkish. Suffice it to say that these spiritual practices carry the wisdom of a great tradition and genuine spiritual path. Consequently, they have clear resonance with, and even overlap with, the insights and spiritual disciplines proposed by Ignatius of Loyola.[8]

---

8 Another very interesting paper would be on the complementary and overlapping insights of Ignatius and Gülen on eliciting great desires, discernment, spiritual freedom, and decision-making.

In a very abridged summary, Sufism includes the following:

- Reaching true belief in God's Divine Oneness and living in accordance with its demands.
- Heeding the Divine Speech (the Qur'ân), discerning and then obeying the commands of the Divine Power and Will as they relate to the universe (the laws of creation and life).
- Overflowing with divine Love and getting along with all other beings realizing that the universe is a cradle of brotherhood.
- Giving precedence to the well-being of others.
- Being open to love, spiritual yearning, delight, and ecstasy.
- Struggling against worldly ambitions and illusions, which lead us to believe that this world is eternal.

Gülen's main goal was to reestablish Sufism on the basis of the Qur'ân and Sunna. He emphasized religious activism, replacing traditional Sufi passivism, asceticism, and exclusive focus on the inner work, with purification of the self through continuous struggle and action within the community — always under the direct guidance of the Qur'ân and Sunna.[9] An overarching realization motivated him: "Humanity has reached a crossroads: one leads to despair, the other to salvation. May God give us the wisdom to make the right choice."[10]

Ignatius viewed himself as a layman seeking to help others through spiritual conversation and spiritual healing, while Gülen dwelt among sages and philosophers and articulated a new path for contemporary Islam. Ignatius inspired a coherent band of followers, who became the Society of Jesus and spread throughout the then-known world to

---

[9] Mustafa Gökçek, "Gülen and Sufism," http://gülenconference.net/files/Rice/MGokcek.pdf, 1.

[10] "Voice of Compassion and Love," *Key Concepts in the Practice of Sufism* (Somerset, NJ: The Light, 2004): *v.* Today, in the United States, there are 28 Jesuit colleges and universities and 46 secondary schools. Currently there are 1,000,000 living alumni who have graduated from an American Jesuit college or university and more than 300,000 living alumni of American Jesuit high schools. In addition to this, since the late 1980s, the Society of Jesus has opened a number of middle schools for minority students throughout the United States. Worldwide, there are 90 Jesuit colleges in 27 countries from El Salvador to Indonesia and 430 secondary schools in 55 countries from Egypt to Japan.

preach the Gospel of Jesus Christ.[11] Gülen has inspired millions to support each other with religious devotion and material sustenance, and move out to the world with a dynamic, new brand of education and scientific endeavor. Both drew deeply on their respective mystical and religious traditions, which is our beginning point.

Mystical and Religious Roots

Born in 1491 to minor nobility in Basque country, Spain, Ignatius lived a worldly life of a courtier until he was severely wounded in battle (1521) and had a profound religious conversion during his convalescence. Even at this stage, he noticed how God was "instructing him as a school boy," guiding him through "diverse spirits" to a greater truth and reality in his life. This discernment of spirits became central to his entire spirituality and led to his deep appreciation for both the affective and rational life.

Thereafter, Ignatius set out on a pilgrim's quest through Spain to Jerusalem during which time he had increasingly profound mystical experiences. Along the River Cardoner in Spain in 1522, for instance, he experienced visions and illuminations so strong that years later, he described his experience "as such that in the whole course of his life, through sixty-two years ... even if he gathered up all the many helps he had had from God and all the many things he knew and added them together, he does not think they would amount to as much as he had received at that one time."[12]

Ignatius never revealed exactly what the vision was, but it seems it was an encounter with God in his essence so that all creation was seen in a new light and acquired a new meaning. It led Ignatius to experience what enabled Ignatius to find God in all things. This grace of finding God in all things is one of the central characteristics of Jesuit spirituality."[13]

[11] John C. Olin, *Autobiography*, (New York: Fordham University Press, 1992): 39-40.
[12] Fr. S.J. Norman O'Neal, *A Brief Life of Ignatius*, http://norprov.org/spirituality/lifeofignatius.htm
[13] John W. O'Malley, *The First Jesuits* (Cambridge, Massachusetts: Harvard University Press, 1993): 27.

In his early quest for an education in Spain, he lived extremely simply, begging for his sustenance, and he also began to guide a few people with the *Spiritual Exercises*, a guide he had developed out of his own mystical experiences in prayer. The *Exercises* recognize that not only intellect but also emotions and feelings can help a person come to a knowledge of the action of the Spirit in his or her life.

Ignatius and his companions also taught catechism to "the great number of people" who assembled, to hear him. Rumors soon spread that these "sack wearers" were in fact *alumbrados*, the "enlightened ones," who were adherents to a movement that extolled the seeking of spiritual perfection through internal illumination. Fearful authorities pursued the *alumbrados* as pseudo mystics who belittled traditional expressions of piety. Several times Ignatius and his friends were brought to the attention of the Inquisition of Toledo, which led to him spending several days in prison. Although they were found innocent, they were admonished not to speak in public on religious matters until they had completed four more years of study.[14]

Several times during the first 100 years of the Jesuits, Catholic authorities expressed serious doubts about the orthodoxy of their spirituality and religious practice. It seemed to smack of Lutheranism or other approaches to God considered heterodox.

After Ignatius and his closest six companions had completed their advanced studies at the University of Paris, they decided to go to the Holy Land "to convert the infidels," or if they failed to do that, to go to Rome and offer themselves to the Pope to be sent (missioned) anywhere in the world. On the way, just outside Rome, Ignatius had his second most significant mystical experience. At a chapel at La Storta, where they had stopped to pray, God the Father told Ignatius, "I will be favorable to you in Rome," and Ignatius experienced himself being placed with Jesus carrying his cross.

Ignatius did not know what this transcendent experience meant, for it could mean persecution as well as success, since Jesus experienced both, but he felt comforted since, as St. Paul wrote, to be with

---

[14] O'Neal, *A Brief Life of Ignatius*, norprov.org/spirituality

Jesus even in persecution was success. When they met with the Pope, the Pope happily put them to work teaching scripture, theology, and preaching.[15] Underlying the journey of Ignatius was a flexibility and willingness to change course if obstacles, such as the war between the Venetians and Turks, made his vision impossible.

Gülen's religious formation does not appear to have had such dramatic points of conversion. Rather, he imbibed the spiritual traditions of his family, such as his father's passion for knowledge and his love of the companions of the Prophet. Early on Gülen was influenced by a family friend who was a local Sufi sheikh, Mehmed Lutfi. As Gülen points out, "His home was like a guesthouse for all knowledgeable and spiritually evolved people in the region."[16] The major philosophical influence on Gülen's thoughts, not only about Sufism but on an overall approach to religion and its application in modern life, came from Bediüz-zaman Said Nursi and his works collected as Risale-i-Nur. According to Gülen, Nursi was his "mind maker" (*beyin yapıcımız*).[17]

Over many years Gülen inspired an increasingly broad band of followers. His strongest appeal was that he is an educator not only of the mind but also of the heart and spirit. "The main duty and purpose of human life," he said, "is to seek understanding."[18] He continued:

> At birth, the outset of the earthly phase of our journey from the world of spirits to eternity, we are wholly impotent and needy ... Our principal duty of life is to acquire perfection and purity in our thinking, conceptions, and belief. By fulfilling our duty of servanthood to the Creator, Nourisher, and Protector, and by penetrating the mystery of creation ... we attain the rank of true humanity and become worthy of a blissful, eternal life, in another, exalted world."[19]

---

[15] Ali Ünal and Alphonse Williams, *Fethullah Gülen: Advocate of Dialogue*, (Fairfax, Virginia: The Fountain, 2000): 11.

[16] Herein I have summarized some excellent material from Mustafa Gökçek, "Gülen and Sufism," http://gülenconference.net/files/Rice/MGokcek.pdf

[17] Gülen, *M.F. Gülen*, 57

[18] Ibid.

[19] Ibid., 58, 77

He concluded, "Our humanity is directly proportional to our emo-tion's purity ... Almost everyone can train their bodies, but few can edu-cate their minds and feelings." Each of us has a spirit, Gülen explains, that needs satisfaction, which is possible only through knowledge of God and belief in Him. Confined to the physical world, the human spirit experiences life as a dungeon.

It's evident that the strength of Ignatius and his followers, and sim-ilarly the strength of Gülen and his followers, rests on their profound grasp of a more intimate, more mystical, more contemporary approach to God. From this experiential basis and transformative effect of reli-gion flows a tremendous dynamic force for creating strong communi-ties of support and for educating youth to be leaders for peace and jus-tice in the world today.

A Practical Mysticism That Values Experience and Takes Action

Both Ignatius and Gülen put a strong emphasis on **experience** and **action.**

In his time Ignatius put a great emphasis on *contemplation in action.* One's own prayer and experiences of God were not for one's self, but for others. Unlike other religious orders until that time, such as the Benedictines and Dominicans, Ignatius meant for his followers to be shakers and movers in the world. Ignatius envisioned reciprocity between prayer and action. Prayer led to direct action, and action led to more prayer.

One of the descriptors most often used for Ignatius was that he was a *practical mystic.* Unlike other founders of Catholic religious orders, such as Francis or Dominic, Ignatius had a great sense for how to inspire, build, and sustain institutions. From the time of the founding of the Jesuits in 1541 until his death in 1556, Ignatius largely sat at his desk answering correspondence and writing out detailed *Constitutions* for how Jesuits were to conduct themselves and how they were to go about founding and running parishes, schools, retreat centers, and houses of formation. Of all the figures of 16th-century Europe, Ignatius had the largest extent of correspondence — more than 7,000 letters. Of these, fully one third are about building schools, securing endowments, gaining the approval of local authorities, and architectural plans. He was not only a mystic, but also a practical man of action.

Likewise, Fethullah Gülen, though a philosopher and a Muslim steeped in the Sufi tradition, was a man of action. He did not retreat from the world, which was a typical trait of Sufism, but rather, he fully engaged the world in all its dimensions. Similar to Ignatius who embraced the best available knowledge and wisdom of his time, especially Renaissance humanism, Gülen values the best of contemporary education. He particularly favors science as an exploration of the mysteries of human nature and the dark areas of existence. Gülen explains, "Since 'real' life is possible only through knowledge, those who neglect learning and teaching are considered 'dead' even though they are still alive. We were created to learn and communicate what we have learned to others."

Despite the disasters caused by science and technology — their mistaken approach to the truth — Gülen finds the fault lies with the scientists who avoid their responsibility; they "cause science to develop in a materialistic atmosphere." They have not remained aware of their social responsibility, and he critiques the West, where, he says in somewhat of an oversimplification, "the Church forced science to develop in opposition to religion."[20] Though Gülen places an extremely high value on science and technology, at heart he is a thorough humanist, a Renaissance man. Art, poetry, culture, literature, philosophy, and religion are all realms of discovery for him. For instance, he says, "Art is the spirit of progress and one of the most important means of developing feelings. Those who cannot make use of art are unfortunate, and live a numbed, diminished life." In addition, he says, "Art is like a magical key that opens hidden treasures. Behind the doors it opens are ideas embodied and dreams given substantial form." Similarly, "Literature," for Gülen, "is the eloquent language of a nation's spiritual composition,

---

[20] A series of pithy sayings of Gülen drawn from *Gülen: Advocate of Dialogue*, 79-94.

world of ideas, and culture. They who do not share this 'language' cannot understand each other, even if they belong to the same nation."[21]

The effect of Gülen has been enormous. More than a decade ago, a Turkish commentator said, "Everyone taking a breath in this country should accept that there is a Fethullah Gülen reality in Turkey. This reality is growing like an avalanche ... Its name is said to be love of humanity."[22] Gülen is most prominently known both within and outside of Turkey for his deep regard of *dialogue* as a way of discovery for truth. Gülen and his followers promoted dialogue, starting in the 1990s especially, as an attempt to bridge divided groups in Turkey, such as "Right-Left" (*Sağcı-Solcu*). In addition, Gülen met and established continuing relations with Turkish Orthodox Patriarch Bartholomeos and Israel's Sephardic head Rabbi Eliyahu Doron, among many other religious leaders. He especially values interreligious dialogue as a means for bringing about peace, a deeper understanding of the human mystery, and of the reality of the Divine Creator.

Both Ignatius in his time and Gülen in contemporary Turkey experienced radical criticism from groups that were threatened by this new, vibrant approach to religious experience and education. In both cases, religious authorities critiqued their spiritual experience and expression of religious truth as deviant from the accepted orthodoxy.

Encouraging and Building Community

Almost every Jesuit university or high school website demonstrates a strong emphasis on encouraging and building community. This emphasis also reflects the Catholic vision of the dignity of every human being *realized in community*. The Catholic vision is not one of "everyone for themselves" or of a highly skilled "individualism" that is so often characteristic of Western capitalism. Rather, it looks to the social network of relationships, which seeks to achieve human flourishing by building

---

[21] Reported by Memduh Bayraktaroğlu in *Akşam* (January 30, 1997).
[22] M. Fethullah Gülen, *Sufism: Key Concepts in the Practice of Sufism* (Somerset NJ: The Light, 2004): iv.

and supporting faith communities in which every human being is accepted, supported, and appreciated.

Some of my Turkish friends, involved in the Gülen movement, have helped me understand their experience of community. In this case, the terms for "community" in Turkish embody a deeper and broader understanding than a simple translation would. The media, for instance, describes the Gülen Movement as a *Cemaat,* which literally means a "group of people gathered at a place." Currently in Turkey, it is used to refer to "a group of people that share the same ideals in practicing Islam, and generally have a leader." However, Gülen refrained from calling the movement a *cemaat* since he doesn't see himself as a leader, but maybe an inspirer. Within the movement, the term for community most commonly used is *dayanışma,* which means "community support," or to be more precise, "members of a community supporting each other." A Turkish friend in Seattle gave me an example of *dayanışma*: When his father had a heart attack, my friend quickly flew home to Turkey. While he was still traveling, he received a text message saying that the entire *dayanışma* was praying for him. He felt immensely supported, "as if we were all leaning into each other for support."

Still another term for the Gülen community, *hizmet,* literally means "service towards others," and is an obvious result of *dayanışma.* So the very naming — *dayanışma* and *hizmet* — are indicative of the deeper spirituality motivating the Gülen community, and these terms likewise portray the dynamic, action-oriented sense of the Gülen movement. This community vision is also fundamental for education. It isn't just for individual achievement, but rather, education is always for others and at the service of the larger community.

Conclusion: The Impact of Spirituality, Action, and Community on Contemporary Education

I have briefly explored three foundational features for contemporary Jesuit and Gülen education. First, the spiritual/mystical roots of both founders suggest that discerning the ways that God is acting in and through creation and through every individual not only enhance education, but provide the inspiration and day-to-day motivation for excellence in teaching.

Secondly, insight without action is worthless. Effective action, in turn, leads to an urgency for contemplation and prayer. Gülen puts it this way: "There is a mutually supportive and perfective relation between an individual's actions and his inner life. We may call it a 'virtuous circle.'"[23] Both Ignatius and Gülen, each in their own right, were men of action. They harnessed the inspirations of Christianity and Sufi Islam to create communities of action in which the talented and the weak were equally supported and affirmed. Ignatius simply expressed it as, "Love overflows into action."

Third and finally, community is vital and foundational for both educational enterprises. For Ignatius, community is a mystical expression of the Living Body of Christ. It is the Communion of Saints — those holy men and women already enjoying the fullness of life with God, as well as those still on Earth. Community is celebrated in Eucharist, the thanksgiving and *communion* of the faithful. The Latin root of community is *cum + unio* that is, "union with." Ignatius used the phrase "Company of Jesus" for his first companions. The Latin roots of company are *cum + panis,* literally "with bread." Figuratively, it means those you "break bread with," those with whom you celebrate life through eating and drinking.

Anyone familiar with the Gülen communities will immediately notice the similarities. These are gatherings of great hospitality and incredible interfaith dialogue, and they are notable for their wonderful food from many different cultures and ethnic groups. The food itself becomes a symbol of the union to which all aspire. Gülen's profound affirmation of a world community occurs in many instances. Let this one suffice: He says that a person's mind and heart are like a honeycomb. "Only the honey of faith, virtue, love of humanity, and all creatures for the sake of the Creator, helping others, self-sacrifice to the extent of foregoing the passion of life to enable others to live, and service to all creation flow from this honeycomb." (FOOTNOTE?) This intricate network brings peace and salvation. It represents the Heaven to which we are headed.

---

[23] Gülen, *M.F. Gülen,* 82

Works Cited

Gülen, M. Fethullah. *M.F. Gülen: Essays, Perspectives, Opinions.* Compiled by The Fountain.Rutherford, NJ: The Light, Inc., 2002.

Woodrow, Alain. "Islam's Moderate Pioneers." *The Tablet*, 2009.

Gökçek, Mustafa. "Gülen and Sufism." http://gülenconference.net/files/Rice/MGokcek.pdf.

"Voice of Compassion and Love," *Key Concepts in the Practice of Sufism*. Somerset, NJ: The Light, 2004.

Olin, John C. *Autobiography.* ed. trans. by Joseph F. O'Callaghan. New York: Fordham University Press, 1992.

O'Neal, Fr. S.J. Norman. *A Brief Life of Ignatius.* http://norprov.org/spirituality/lifeofignatius.htm

O'Malley, John W. *The First Jesuits.* Cambridge, Massachusetts: Harvard University Press, 1993.

Ünal, Ali, and Alphonse Williams. *Fethullah Gülen: Advocate of Dialogue.* Fairfax, Virginia: The Fountain, 2000.

Gülen, M. Fethullah. *Sufism: Key Concepts in the Practice of Sufism.* Somerset NJ: The Light, 2004.